3D Modeling & Print with Artificial Intelligence

- A Roadmap to Start Million Dollar Business

Dr. V. Hanuman Kumar, Ph.D

NOTION PRESS

Dedicated to My Family

"Anuhya" & "Dhatrika"

And Parents

Vudata Leela Krishna Babu

Padmavathi

Contents

Foreword

Dr. V. Hanuman Kumar is a certified data science and machine learning professional, academician, author and has strong research expertise in computer science engineering. Dr. Hanuman authored research articles on artificial intelligence, machine learning, data science, computerized bionics and python programming. He worked with various machine learing algorithms with the advent of data science concepts to solve business problems. In authors works the major area of concern is data science with python programming language.

Additive manufacturing (AM), commonly known as 3D printing has undergone significant evolution since its inception. This innovative technology has transformed from a niche prototyping tool to a mainstream manufacturing process with diverse applications across various industries. The journey of additive manufacturing can be traced through several key phases:

1. The Birth of Additive Manufacturing (1980s)

Early Innovations:

- The concept of additive manufacturing emerged in the 1980s. The earliest patents for stereolithography (SLA) were filed by Charles Hull in 1984, which laid the groundwork for modern 3D printing. SLA uses ultraviolet lasers to solidify photopolymer resins layer by layer.

- In 1986, Hull co-founded 3D Systems, which introduced the first commercial 3D printer, the SLA-1.

2. Expansion and Diversification (1990s)

Introduction of New Technologies:

- The 1990s saw the development of various 3D printing technologies. Selective Laser Sintering (SLS), developed by Carl Deckard and patented in 1989, used lasers to fuse powdered materials.

- Fused Deposition Modeling (FDM), developed by S. Scott Crump in 1988 and commercialized by Stratasys, became popular for its affordability and ease of use.

Prototyping and Tooling:

- During this period, AM was primarily used for rapid prototyping and tooling. It enabled designers and engineers to create functional prototypes quickly, accelerating product development cycles.

3. Commercialization and Growth (2000s)

Industrial Applications:

- The 2000s marked the commercialization of additive manufacturing for industrial applications. Companies began using AM for creating end-use parts in industries such as aerospace, automotive, and healthcare.

- The introduction of metal 3D printing technologies, such as Direct Metal Laser Sintering (DMLS) and Electron Beam Melting (EBM), expanded the capabilities of AM to include high-strength, complex metal parts.

Open Source Movement:

- The RepRap project, initiated by Dr. Adrian Bowyer in 2005, played a crucial role in democratizing 3D printing. RepRap aimed to create a self-replicating 3D printer, leading to the proliferation of open-source 3D printers and a thriving maker community.

4. Mainstream Adoption and Technological Advancements (2010s)

Consumer 3D Printing:

- The 2010s saw a surge in consumer-grade 3D printers, making the technology accessible to hobbyists and small businesses. Companies like MakerBot popularized desktop 3D printers, enabling users to create custom objects at home.

- The rise of online platforms, such as Thingiverse and Shapeways, facilitated the sharing and commercialization of 3D printable designs.

Advancements in Materials:

- Significant advancements were made in the development of new materials, including high-performance polymers, composites, and bio-compatible materials. This broadened the range of applications for AM in sectors like healthcare (e.g., custom implants and prosthetics) and fashion (e.g., customized clothing and accessories).

5. Integration with Digital Technologies (2020s and Beyond)

Artificial Intelligence and Machine Learning:

- The integration of AI and machine learning is revolutionizing additive manufacturing. AI algorithms optimize design for manufacturability, predict failures, and enhance quality control, making the production process more efficient and reliable.

Industry 4.0:

- Additive manufacturing is a key component of Industry 4.0, characterized by the integration of digital technologies, IoT, and automation. Smart factories leverage AM for on-demand production, reducing lead times and minimizing inventory costs.

- The use of digital twins, virtual models of physical objects, allows for real-time monitoring and optimization of the manufacturing process.

Sustainability and Customization:

- AM contributes to sustainable manufacturing by reducing material waste and enabling localized production, which minimizes transportation emissions. Customization and personalization of products are also becoming more prevalent, catering to individual consumer needs.

The evolution of additive manufacturing has been marked by continuous innovation and expanding applications. From its early days as a rapid prototyping tool to its current role in mainstream manufacturing, AM has significantly impacted various industries. The future promises even greater advancements as additive manufacturing integrates with emerging technologies like artificial intelligence, driving the next wave of industrial revolution and opening new frontiers for creativity and production.

The author's work in this book will definitely create a roadmap to start business in additive manufacturing

Prasad Mani
Project Manager,
Movate Technologies, Chennai
04-07-2024

Preface

"3D Modeling & Print with Artificial Intelligence – A Roadmap to Start Million Dollar Business" serves as a crucial guide for entrepreneurs, engineers, and business leaders seeking to harness the transformative power of 3D printing and AI. This comprehensive book delves into the synergies between additive manufacturing (AM) and artificial intelligence (AI), illustrating how these technologies are revolutionizing industries and creating unparalleled business opportunities. This book also serves to start your business in additive manufacturing with the integration of advanced technologies like artificial intelligence.

Dr. V. Hanuman Kumar

04-07-2024

Acknowledgments

It is my privilege to convey sincere thanks to Mr. Ashok Raja and Mr. Meenakshi Sundar, Delivery Head, International Flavours and Fragnances, Chennai, for their support during my professional journey.

It's time to convey my gratitude to Dr. Sivaram Prasad, HOD, and Dept. Of IT, Bapatla Engineering College, Bapatla

I am very much desire to convey acknowledges to my parents for their love and effection

1. FOUNDATION

1.1.   Additive Manufacturing

The world of manufacturing has undergone a seismic shift in recent decades, largely driven by the rise of Additive Manufacturing (AM). This revolutionary technology, often referred to as 3D printing, is reshaping industries across the board.

Additive manufacturing, at its core, is the process of creating an object by building it one layer at a time. This is fundamentally different from traditional manufacturing, which relies on subtractive methods, cutting away material from a solid block to achieve the desired shape.

The concept of Additive Manufacturing can be traced back to the 1980s when Dr. Hideo Kodama, a Japanese researcher, developed an early version of a 3D printing process called "stereo lithography." Around the same time, American engineer Charles Hull invented the "stereo lithography apparatus" (SLA) and co-founded 3D Systems Corporation, which played a pivotal role in popularizing the technology.

Advancements in materials, printing technologies, and affordability led to a broader range of applications beyond its initial use in prototyping. Industries such as aerospace, automotive, healthcare, and consumer goods started to explore the potential of additive manufacturing.

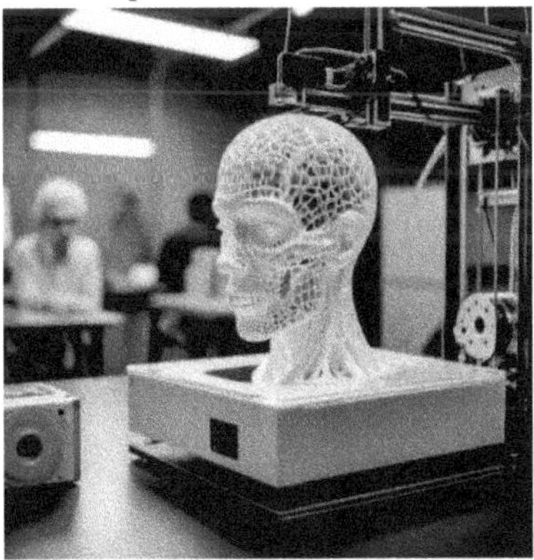

Fig.1.1 Additive manufacturing system

In the world of 3D printing, the future is already here, and it's set to reshape how we think about design and manufacturing. As 3D printing technology becomes more accessible and user-friendly, designers will have greater creative freedom. AI-driven tools will assist in creating optimized designs, making complex geometries and efficient structures achievable with ease.

Traditional manufacturing methods, including subtractive techniques and molding processes, have been the backbone of the production industry for many years. However, these methods come with inherent drawbacks. Firstly, subtractive techniques often lead to material wastage since they involve removing materials from a larger block to create the desired part. This not only increases the cost of production but also the environmental footprint. Mold-based processes, on the other hand, demand significant upfront investments in creating molds, making them cost-inefficient for low-volume or customized productions. Furthermore, traditional methods can restrict design freedom, complicating the production of intricate geometries and internal structures.

1.2. Why is it called Additive Manufacturing?

The etymology of the term "additive manufacturing" comes from the methodical contrast between how 3D printing and traditional "subtractive" manufacturing processes work to shape objects. 3D printers work through the addition of layers of material in different shapes on top of each other. Traditional manufacturing methods produce the final result through the reduction or subtraction of material, such as cutting away sections of an alloy to make a bolt or hinge. Traditional subtractive manufacturing is notoriously slow, expensive, and comes with design limitations, whereas additive manufacturing is paving the way for quick, low-cost, automated processes.

ASPECT	3D PRINTING	TRADITIONAL MANUFACTURING
Method	Additive; builds layer by layer	Subtractive; often removes material
Flexibility	High; easy to customize designs	Lower; customization is more complex
Speed	Faster for prototypes and small runs	Slower for prototypes, faster for large-scale production
Cost	Lower for small runs and prototypes	Economically efficient for mass production
Waste	Minimal; material is added as needed	Higher; excess material is often removed and discarded
Design Constraints	Fewer; complex designs are feasible	More; limited by tooling and machining capabilities
Material Variety	Wide range, including plastics and metals	Usually specific to the manufacturing process
Environmental Impact	Generally lower	Higher due to waste and energy usage in mass production
Application	Prototyping, custom parts, complex structures	Mass production, standardized parts

Table 1. Additive manufacturing Vs Traditional manufacturing

1.3.   Additive Manufacturing Techniques:

Additive manufacturing, commonly known as 3D printing, encompasses a variety of processes used to create objects by adding material layer by layer, as opposed to traditional subtractive manufacturing which removes material.

Here are some of the primary techniques in detail:

1. Fused Deposition Modeling (FDM) / Fused Filament Fabrication (FFF)

- **Process:** A thermoplastic filament is heated and extruded through a nozzle to build an object layer by layer.
- **Materials:** PLA, ABS, PETG, nylon, and other thermoplastics.
- **Applications:** Prototyping, hobbyist projects, and manufacturing of end-use parts.
- **Advantages:** Cost-effective, wide material availability, ease of use.
- **Disadvantages:** Lower resolution and surface finish compared to other methods, anisotropic mechanical properties.

2. Stereo lithography (SLA)

- **Process:** A laser cures and solidifies layers of photopolymer resin in a vat, building the object layer by layer.
- **Materials:** Photopolymer resins.
- **Applications:** High-detail prototypes, molds, jewelry, dental models.
- **Advantages:** High resolution and surface finish, good for intricate designs.
- **Disadvantages:** More expensive, limited material properties, post-processing required removing supports and curing the resin.

3. Selective Laser Sintering (SLS)

- **Process:** A laser sinters powdered material (usually nylon) layer by layer to form an object.
- **Materials:** Nylon, polyamides, thermoplastic elastomers, metals, and ceramics.
- **Applications:** Functional prototypes, small production runs, complex geometries.
- **Advantages:** No need for support structures, good mechanical properties, functional parts.
- **Disadvantages:** Rough surface finish, limited to specific materials, expensive equipment.

4. Digital Light Processing (DLP)

- **Process:** Similar to SLA, but uses a digital light projector screens to flash a single image of each layer all at once, curing the resin.
- **Materials:** Photopolymer resins.
- **Applications:** Jewelry, dental applications, high-detail prototypes.
- **Advantages:** High resolution and surface finish, faster than SLA.
- **Disadvantages:** Limited material properties, post-processing required.

5. Material Jetting

- **Process:** Droplets of material (usually photopolymer) are deposited layer by layer and cured using UV light.
- **Materials:** Photopolymers waxes.

- **Applications:** High-detail prototypes, casting patterns, medical models.
- **Advantages:** High resolution, ability to print multiple materials and colors.
- **Disadvantages:** Expensive, limited to specific materials, parts can be brittle.

6. Binder Jetting

- **Process:** A binding agent is selectively deposited onto a powder bed, bonding the material layer by layer.
- **Materials:** Metals, ceramics, sand, and composites.
- **Applications:** Sand casting molds, metal parts (post-processing required), prototypes.
- **Advantages:** No thermal stresses, can use a wide range of materials.
- **Disadvantages:** Parts are often porous and may require infiltration or sintering.

7. Direct Metal Laser Sintering (DMLS) / Selective Laser Melting (SLM)

- **Process:** A laser melts and fuses metallic powder layer by layer.
- **Materials:** Titanium, stainless steel, aluminum, cobalt-chrome, and other metal alloys.
- **Applications:** Aerospace, medical implants, complex metal parts.
- **Advantages:** High strength and density, complex geometries possible.
- **Disadvantages:** Expensive, requires support structures and post-processing.

8. Electron Beam Melting (EBM)

- **Process:** Similar to DMLS/SLM, but uses an electron beam to melt the metal powder.
- **Materials:** Titanium alloys, cobalt-chrome.
- **Applications:** Aerospace, medical implants, structural parts.
- **Advantages:** High energy efficiency, capable of producing high-density parts.
- **Disadvantages:** Expensive, limited material availability, vacuum environment required.

9. Laminated Object Manufacturing (LOM)

- **Process:** Layers of adhesive-coated paper, plastic, or metal laminates are successively glued together and cut to shape.
- **Materials:** Paper, plastic, metal foil.
- **Applications:** Prototypes, concept models.
- **Advantages:** Low material costs, large parts possible.
- **Disadvantages:** Lower resolution and surface finish, limited material properties.

10. Directed Energy Deposition (DED)

- **Process:** Focused thermal energy (laser, electron beam, or plasma arc) is used to fuse materials by melting them as they are being deposited.
- **Materials:** Metals, metal alloys.
- **Applications:** Repair of existing parts, adding features to existing parts, complex geometries.
- **Advantages:** Ability to repair and add material to existing parts, high material deposition rates.
- **Disadvantages:** Requires complex machinery and control systems, limited to specific materials.

1.4.   3D – Modeling

3D modeling is the process of creating a three-dimensional representation of any object or surface using specialized software. This digital object can be viewed, edited, and manipulated on a computer. Here's a detailed look at the 3D modeling process:

1. Software and Tools

- **Software:** Popular 3D modeling software includes Blender, Autodesk Maya, Autodesk 3ds Max, Tinkercad, SolidWorks, Rhino, and SketchUp.
- **Tools:** This software provide various tools for creating and manipulating 3D models, such as extrusion, lofting, subdivision surfaces, Boolean operations, and more.

2. Modeling Techniques

- **Polygonal Modeling:** The most common technique, using polygons (triangles, quads, or other multi-sided shapes) to build the model. Each polygon consists of vertices, edges, and faces.

- **NURBS Modeling:** Uses mathematical representations (Non-Uniform Rational B-Splines) to create smooth and precise curves and surfaces.
- **Sculpting:** Allows for more organic shapes by pushing, pulling, and molding the mesh, similar to clay sculpting. Software like ZBrush is popular for this.
- **Parametric Modeling:** Used in CAD software, where models are defined by parameters and mathematical functions, allowing for precise control and modifications.
- **Procedural Modeling:** Uses algorithms and rules to automatically generate complex structures and patterns.

3. Workflow

1. **Conceptualization:** Define the idea or object to be modeled.
2. **Sketching:** Create rough sketches or reference images.
3. **Blocking:** Create the basic shapes and structure of the model.
4. **Detailing:** Add finer details to the model, refining shapes and surfaces.
5. **Texturing and Shading:** Apply materials and textures to give the model color, surface detail, and realistic appearance.
6. **Rigging (optional):** For animated models, create a skeleton and define how the model moves.
7. **Rendering:** Generate images or animations of the 3D model for visualization.

1.5.   3D – Printing

3D printing is an additive manufacturing process that creates physical objects from digital models by adding material layer by layer. Here's a detailed explanation of the 3D printing process:

1. Preparation

- **3D Model Creation:** The digital model is created using 3D modeling software or scanned from an existing object.
- **File Format:** The model is exported in a format suitable for 3D printing, typically STL (Stereo lithography) or OBJ.
- **Slicing:** The 3D model is sliced into thin horizontal layers using slicing software (e.g., Cura, PrusaSlicer). The software also generates G-code, which instructs the printer on how to build the object layer by layer.

2. Printing Process

- **Printer Setup:** Set up the 3D printer, including loading the material (filament, resin, powder, etc.) and preparing the build platform.
- **Calibration:** Calibrate the printer to ensure accurate dimensions and proper adhesion of the first layer.
- **Printing:** Start the print job. The printer follows the G-code instructions, depositing material layer by layer to build the object.

3. Post-Processing

- **Removal:** Carefully remove the printed object from the build platform.
- **Cleaning:** Remove any support structures or excess material.
- **Finishing:** Depending on the material and desired quality, additional finishing steps may include sanding, polishing, painting, or coating.
- **Curing (for resin prints):** UV curing to harden and strengthen the printed object.

Common 3D Printing Technologies

- **Fused Deposition Modeling (FDM):** Uses a thermoplastic filament that is melted and extruded through a nozzle.
- **Stereo lithography (SLA):** Uses a laser to cure liquid resin layer by layer.
- **Selective Laser Sintering (SLS):** Uses a laser to sinter powdered material.
- **Digital Light Processing (DLP):** Uses a projector to cure resin layer by layer.
- **Material Jetting:** Jets droplets of material which are cured by UV light.
- **Binder Jetting:** Uses a binding agent to join powder particles.
- **Direct Metal Laser Sintering (DMLS) / Selective Laser Melting (SLM):** Uses a laser to melt and fuse metal powder.

1.6. Applications

3D modeling and 3D printing are revolutionizing many industries by enabling rapid prototyping, custom manufacturing, and the creation of complex and intricate designs that are not feasible with traditional manufacturing methods.

Fig.1.2 Top 10 Applications of 3D printing

1. Prototyping and Product Development

- **Concept Models:** Rapid creation of physical models to visualize and communicate design ideas.
- **Functional Prototypes:** Test form, fit, and function of products before mass production.
- **Iterative Design:** Quick modifications and reprints to refine designs based on feedback.

2. Manufacturing

- **Tooling and Fixtures:** Custom tools, jigs, and fixtures to aid in the manufacturing process.
- **End-Use Parts:** Small batch production of parts, especially for complex geometries and low-volume needs.
- **Customization:** Personalized products tailored to individual specifications.

3. Healthcare and Medicine

- **Medical Implants:** Custom implants tailored to patients' anatomy, such as dental implants, hip joints, and cranial plates.
- **Prosthetics:** Affordable and custom-fit prosthetic limbs and devices.
- **Surgical Guides:** Precise guides for surgeons to plan and execute complex procedures.

- **Anatomical Models:** Detailed models for surgical planning, medical training, and patient education.

4. Aerospace and Defense

- **Lightweight Components:** Manufacture of lightweight, strong parts to reduce aircraft weight and improve fuel efficiency.
- **Complex Geometries:** Production of components with intricate geometries that are difficult or impossible to make with traditional methods.
- **Rapid Repair:** On-site printing of replacement parts and tools for maintenance and repairs.

5. Automotive Industry

- **Prototyping:** Rapid creation of prototypes for new vehicle designs and parts.
- **Tooling:** Custom jigs, fixtures, and assembly tools for the production line.
- **End-Use Parts:** Low-volume production of specialized components, such as racing car parts and custom accessories.

6. Architecture and Construction

- **Scale Models:** Detailed architectural models to visualize buildings and structures.
- **Custom Components:** Unique building elements and decorative features.
- **Construction Printing:** Large-scale 3D printing for building walls, bridges, and other structures.

7. Consumer Goods

- **Custom Products:** Personalized items such as jewelry, eyewear, and fashion accessories.
- **Replacement Parts:** Manufacturing of hard-to-find or obsolete parts for repair and maintenance.
- **Toys and Collectibles:** Production of detailed and custom-designed toys and collectible items.

8. Education and Research

- **Educational Models:** Physical models for teaching complex concepts in science, engineering, and art.
- **Research Prototypes:** Creating prototypes for experimental research and development.

- **Hands-On Learning:** Engaging students in STEM subjects through hands-on design and fabrication projects.

9. Art and Design

- **Sculptures and Installations:** Creating intricate and large-scale art pieces.
- **Product Design:** Developing unique and customized consumer products.
- **Fashion:** Designing and producing wearable art and custom fashion pieces.

10. Entertainment and Media

- **Props and Set Design:** Custom props, costumes, and set pieces for movies, theater, and television.
- **Animation and Gaming:** Creating highly detailed models for visual effects and game characters.
- **Merchandise:** Custom and collectible items for fans and consumers.

11. Food Industry

- **Custom Edibles:** Designing and printing custom chocolates, cakes, and other edible items.
- **Food Production:** Creating molds and tools for food processing and presentation.
- **Novelty Items:** Producing unique and intricate food designs for events and marketing.

12. Environmental and Sustainability Efforts

- **Recycling Initiatives:** Printing with recycled materials to reduce waste.
- **Sustainable Manufacturing:** Producing parts on-demand to minimize overproduction and inventory waste.
- **Eco-Friendly Materials:** Developing and using biodegradable and sustainable materials for printing.

13. Robotics and Automation

- **Custom Parts:** Creating specialized components for robots and automated systems.
- **Rapid Prototyping:** Developing and testing new robotic designs quickly.
- **Integration:** Combining electronic components with 3D printed parts for integrated solutions.

14. Fashion and Textile Industry

- **Custom Clothing:** Designing and printing custom-fit garments and accessories.
- **Textile Printing:** Creating complex and intricate textile patterns and structures.
- **Fashion Accessories:** Producing unique jewelry, shoes, and other fashion items.

15. Sports and Recreation

- **Custom Gear:** Personalized sports equipment and protective gear.
- **Prototypes:** Rapid development and testing of new sports equipment designs.
- **Replacement Parts:** Quick production of replacement parts for sports equipment.

16. Marine and Maritime Industry

- **Custom Components:** Creating specialized parts for boats and marine structures.
- **Repairs:** On-site printing of replacement parts for maritime repairs.
- **Prototyping:** Developing and testing new marine technologies and designs.

3D modeling and printing technology continue to evolve, opening up new possibilities and applications across various fields. Its ability to quickly and cost-effectively produce custom, complex, and functional parts makes it an invaluable tool in modern manufacturing and design.

1.7. Career Opportunities

The fields of additive manufacturing (AM) and 3D modeling/printing offer a variety of job opportunities across numerous industries. As these technologies continue to advance and integrate into more sectors, the demand for skilled professionals is growing. Here are some key job opportunities in these fields:

1. 3D Modeler/Designer

- **Responsibilities:** Creating detailed 3D models for various applications, including product design, architecture, gaming, and more.

- **Skills Required:** Proficiency in 3D modeling software (e.g., Blender, Autodesk Maya, SolidWorks), artistic skills, understanding of design principles.
- **Industries:** Entertainment, product design, architecture, automotive, aerospace, consumer goods.

2. Additive Manufacturing Engineer

- **Responsibilities:** Designing, developing, and optimizing 3D printing processes and systems, material selection, quality control, and troubleshooting.
- **Skills Required:** Knowledge of 3D printing technologies, materials science, mechanical engineering principles, CAD software proficiency.
- **Industries:** Aerospace, automotive, medical devices, manufacturing, research and development.

3. CAD Technician

- **Responsibilities:** Creating technical drawings and models using CAD software for manufacturing, construction, and engineering projects.
- **Skills Required:** Proficiency in CAD software (e.g., AutoCAD, SolidWorks), technical drawing skills, and understanding of engineering and architectural principles.
- **Industries:** Engineering, architecture, manufacturing, construction.

4. 3D Printing Technician/Operator

- **Responsibilities:** Operating and maintaining 3D printers, preparing print files, troubleshooting printing issues, post-processing printed parts.
- **Skills Required:** Familiarity with different 3D printing technologies, mechanical aptitude, attention to detail, problem-solving skills.
- **Industries:** Manufacturing, prototyping, education, research labs.

5. Research Scientist/Engineer

- **Responsibilities:** Conducting research on new materials, processes, and applications for 3D printing, developing innovative solutions, publishing findings.

- **Skills Required:** Advanced degree in a relevant field (materials science, engineering, and chemistry), strong analytical skills, and research experience.
- **Industries:** Academia, R&D departments, government labs, private research firms.

6. Product Development Engineer

- **Responsibilities:** Designing and developing new products using 3D printing technology, from concept through to production.
- **Skills Required:** Knowledge of product design principles, CAD software, 3D printing processes, and project management skills.
- **Industries:** Consumer products, medical devices, automotive, aerospace.

7. Materials Engineer

- **Responsibilities:** Developing and testing new materials for use in 3D printing, optimizing material properties, ensuring quality and performance.
- **Skills Required:** Materials science knowledge, experience with material testing and analysis, understanding of 3D printing technologies.
- **Industries:** Aerospace, automotive, medical devices, manufacturing, R&D.

8. Quality Assurance Engineer

- **Responsibilities:** Ensuring the quality and reliability of 3D printed parts, developing testing protocols, conducting inspections, troubleshooting defects.
- **Skills Required:** Knowledge of quality control principles, experience with testing and inspection methods, problem-solving skills.
- **Industries:** Manufacturing, aerospace, medical devices, automotive.

9. Sales and Marketing Specialist

- **Responsibilities:** Promoting and selling 3D printing services and products, developing marketing strategies, engaging with clients, conducting market research.
- **Skills Required:** Knowledge of 3D printing technologies, strong communication and sales skills, marketing expertise.

- **Industries:** 3D printing service providers, manufacturing, technology companies.

10. Application Engineer

- **Responsibilities:** Providing technical support and solutions to clients using 3D printing technology, demonstrating capabilities, customizing solutions.
- **Skills Required:** Technical knowledge of 3D printing processes, strong problem-solving skills, customer service orientation.
- **Industries:** 3D printing service providers, technology companies, manufacturing.

11. Industrial Designer

- **Responsibilities:** Designing innovative products and solutions using 3D printing, focusing on aesthetics, functionality, and user experience.
- **Skills Required:** Proficiency in design software, creative thinking, understanding of manufacturing processes, user-centered design principles.
- **Industries:** Consumer products, electronics, furniture, automotive.

12. Educator/Trainer

- **Responsibilities:** Teaching and training students or professionals in 3D modeling and printing techniques, developing curriculum, conducting workshops.
- **Skills Required:** In-depth knowledge of 3D modeling and printing technologies, teaching skills, ability to develop educational materials.
- **Industries:** Educational institutions, training centers, corporate training departments.

13. Technical Writer

- **Responsibilities:** Creating manuals, guides, and documentation for 3D printing technologies, software, and processes.
- **Skills Required:** Strong writing and communication skills, technical understanding of 3D printing, ability to explain complex concepts clearly.
- **Industries:** Technology companies, 3D printer manufacturers, software companies.

14. Entrepreneur/Startup Founder

- **Responsibilities:** Starting and managing a business focused on 3D printing services, products, or technology development.
- **Skills Required:** Business acumen, understanding of 3D printing market and technology, innovation, management skills.
- **Industries:** Various, depending on the business model (e.g., service bureau, product development, software development).

15. Service Bureau Manager

- **Responsibilities:** Managing operations of a 3D printing service bureau, overseeing production, ensuring quality, managing customer relationships.
- **Skills Required:** Knowledge of 3D printing technologies, management skills, customer service skills, operational efficiency.
- **Industries:** 3D printing service providers, manufacturing.

As 3D printing and additive manufacturing continue to evolve, new job roles and opportunities will emerge, making it a dynamic and exciting field to be involved in.

2. BUSINESS COMPONENTS

3D modeling and printing encompass a wide range of business components, from the creation of digital models to the production of physical objects. Here's an overview of the key business components involved in this industry.

3D – Print Businesses Ways to Make Money:
3D printing businesses require effort, investment, and skills. Many small businesses offer a combination of products and services. Use these examples to inspire your own business:

- Sell 3D-printed products
- Offer on-demand 3D printing services
- Create 3D-printing-related content
- Sell your designs
- Sell products on Online | Offline
- Drop ship 3D printers, parts, and materials
- Offer 3D printing design consultation
- Use 3D scanners for reverse engineering
- Set up and repair 3D printers

3D – Printers and Applications:
3D printing encompasses several different technologies, each with its unique strengths, suitable materials, and applications.

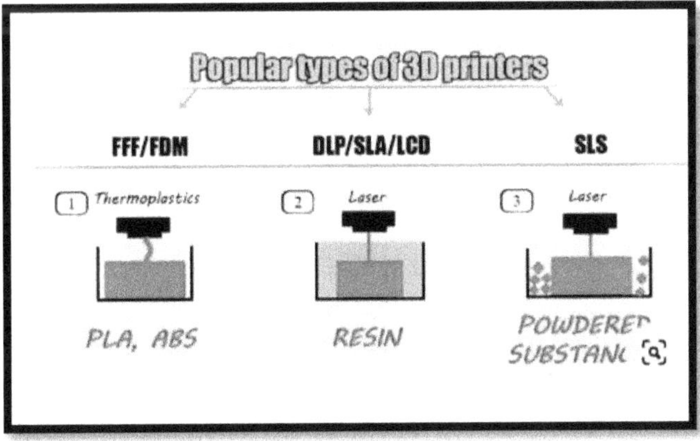

Fig.2.1. Popular types of 3d Printers

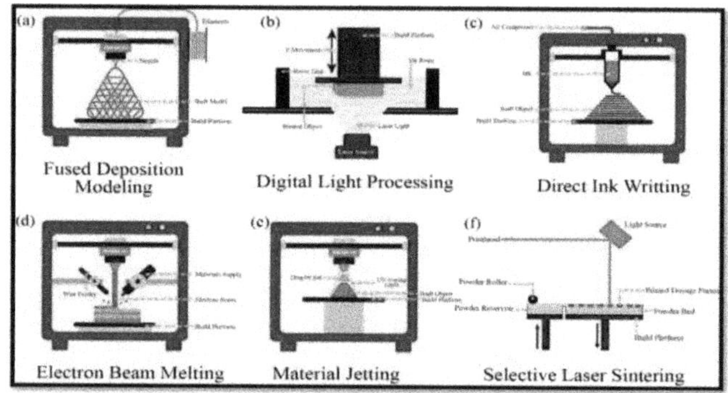

Fig.2.2. Schematic of 3D – Printers

Here's a detailed overview of the main types of 3D printers and their applications:

1. **Fused Deposition Modeling (FDM) / Fused Filament Fabrication (FFF)**

    o **How It Works**: FDM printers use a thermoplastic filament, which is heated to its melting point and then extruded layer by layer to create an object.

    o **Materials**: PLA, ABS, PETG, TPU, and other thermoplastics.

    o **Applications**:

        ▪ Prototyping: Quick and cost-effective creation of prototypes.

        ▪ Consumer Products: Toys, household items, and personalized goods.

        ▪ Educational Tools: Demonstrating concepts and creating models in classrooms.

2. **Stereo lithography (SLA)**

    o **How It Works**: SLA printers use a laser to cure liquid resin into hardened plastic in a layer-by-layer process.

- o **Materials**: Photopolymer resins.

- o **Applications**:

    - High-Detail Prototyping: Detailed prototypes for engineering and design.

    - Dental and Medical Models: Custom dental implants and surgical guides.

    - Jewelry: High-precision models for casting.

3. **Digital Light Processing (DLP)**

   - o **How It Works**: Similar to SLA, but uses a digital light projector screen to flash an image of a layer across the entire resin surface, curing it simultaneously.

   - o **Materials**: Photopolymer resins.

   - o **Applications**:

       - Similar to SLA with a focus on speed and high detail.

       - Miniatures and Detailed Models: Used in industries like jewelry and dental.

4. **Selective Laser Sintering (SLS)**

   - o **How It Works**: SLS printers use a laser to sinter powdered material, binding it together to form a solid structure.

   - o **Materials**: Nylon, TPU, metals, and other powdered materials.

   - o **Applications**:

       - Functional Prototypes: Durable prototypes with complex geometries.

- End-Use Parts: Low-volume production of parts with mechanical properties.

- Aerospace and Automotive: Lightweight and strong components.

5. **Multi Jet Fusion (MJF)**

   o **How It Works**: MJF uses an inkjet array to selectively apply fusing agents to a powder bed, which are then fused by heating elements.

   o **Materials**: Nylon, TPU.

   o **Applications**:

     - Functional Parts: Production of strong and flexible parts.

     - Prototypes: High-quality prototypes with fine details.

     - Short-Run Production: Efficient for low-volume manufacturing.

6. **PolyJet**

   o **How It Works**: PolyJet printers jet layers of curable liquid photopolymer onto a build tray.

   o **Materials**: Photopolymers.

   o **Applications**:

     - High-Resolution Prototypes: Detailed models with smooth surfaces.

     - Medical Models: Anatomically accurate models for surgical planning.

- Multi-Material Prototyping: Parts with different material properties and colors.

7. Direct Metal Laser Sintering (DMLS) / Selective Laser Melting (SLM)

- **How It Works**: These printers use a laser to melt and fuse metallic powders layer by layer.

- **Materials**: Stainless steel, aluminum, titanium, cobalt-chrome, and other metal alloys.

- **Applications**:

    - Aerospace and Automotive: High-strength, lightweight components.

    - Medical Implants: Custom and durable implants and prosthetics.

    - Tooling and Mold Making: Complex tooling inserts and molds.

8. Electron Beam Melting (EBM)

- **How It Works**: EBM uses an electron beam to melt metal powder, layer by layer, to form an object.

- **Materials**: Titanium and other metal alloys.

- **Applications**:

    - Aerospace: High-performance and lightweight parts.

    - Medical Implants: Custom and biocompatible implants.

    - Research and Development: Advanced material studies and prototyping.

3D printing materials are diverse and cater to a wide range of applications, from prototyping and tooling to end-use parts in various industries. Here's an overview of the main types of 3D printing materials and their applications:

3D – Print Materials

3D printing materials can vary widely, with options that include plastic, powders, resins, metal and carbon fiber. These materials make 3D printing a promising option for many parts, from highly accurate aerospace and industrial machinery components to customized consumer goods.

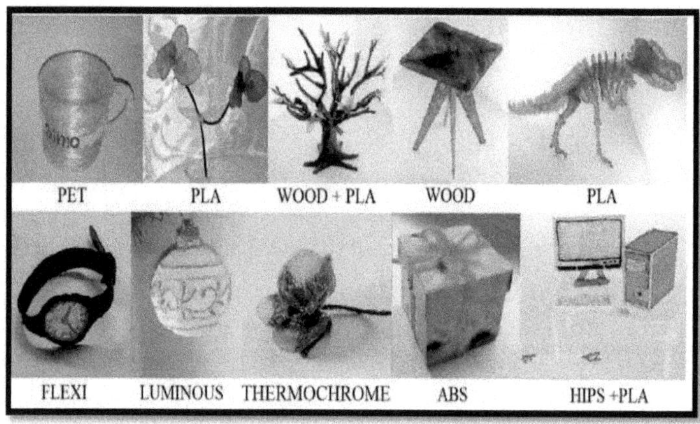

Fig.2.2. 3D – Print material with product sample

1. **Thermoplastics**
   - **PLA (Polylactic Acid)**

     - **Properties**: Biodegradable, easy to print, low warping.

     - **Applications**: Prototypes, educational models, consumer goods.

   - **ABS (Acrylonitrile Butadiene Styrene)**

     - **Properties**: Durable, impact-resistant, can be post-processed easily.

- **Applications**: Automotive parts, electronic housings, toys.

- o **PETG (Polyethylene Terephthalate Glycol)**

  - **Properties**: Strong, flexible, chemical-resistant.

  - **Applications**: Food containers, mechanical parts, protective covers.

- o **TPU (Thermoplastic Polyurethane)**

  - **Properties**: Flexible, durable, rubber-like.

  - **Applications**: Wearables, phone cases, medical devices.

- o **Nylon (Polyamide)**

  - **Properties**: Strong, flexible, abrasion-resistant.

  - **Applications**: Functional prototypes, gears, tools.

2. **Photopolymer Resins**

- o **Standard Resins**

  - **Properties**: High detail, smooth finish, brittle.

  - **Applications**: Detailed prototypes, models, art pieces.

- o **Engineering Resins**

  - **Properties**: Enhanced mechanical properties, heat resistance.

  - **Applications**: Functional prototypes, dental models, medical devices.

- o **Cast able Resins**

- **Properties**: Burns out cleanly, suitable for casting.

- **Applications**: Jewelry, dental crowns, investment casting.

3. **Powders**

   - **Nylon (Polyamide) Powders**

     - **Properties**: Strong, flexible, durable.

     - **Applications**: Functional parts, prototypes, complex geometries.

   - **Metal Powders**

     - **Materials**: Stainless steel, titanium, aluminum, cobalt-chrome.

     - **Applications**: Aerospace parts, medical implants, tooling.

   - **Ceramic Powders**

     - **Properties**: Heat-resistant, hard, brittle.

     - **Applications**: Dental restorations, art, high-temperature applications.

4. **Composites**

   - **Carbon Fiber Reinforced**

     - **Properties**: High strength-to-weight ratio, stiff, lightweight.

     - **Applications**: Aerospace components, automotive parts, sports equipment.

   - **Glass Fiber Reinforced**

- **Properties**: Durable, strong, less brittle than carbon fiber.

- **Applications**: Industrial parts, tools, consumer goods.

  - **Metal-Filled**

    - **Properties**: Metallic finish, added weight, can be polished.

    - **Applications**: Jewelry, decorative items, functional prototypes.

5. **Biomaterials**

   - **Properties**: Biocompatible, suitable for medical applications.

   - **Applications**: Medical implants, tissue engineering, custom prosthetics.

Applications of 3D – Print Materials

1. **Prototyping**

   - **Materials**: PLA, ABS, PETG, standard resins.

   - **Benefits**: Rapid iteration, reduced development costs, early design validation.

2. **Tooling and Fixtures**

   - **Materials**: Nylon, carbon fiber composites, engineering resins.

   - **Benefits**: Custom tools, jigs, and fixtures for manufacturing processes.

3. **End-Use Parts**

- o **Materials**: Metal powders, high-performance thermoplastics (PEEK, ULTEM), nylon.

  - o **Benefits**: Customized production parts, reduced inventory, on-demand manufacturing.

4. **Healthcare**

    - o **Materials**: Biocompatible resins, medical-grade thermoplastics, titanium.

    - o **Applications**: Custom implants, prosthetics, dental models, surgical guides.

5. **Aerospace and Automotive**

    - o **Materials**: Metal powders, high-strength composites, engineering resins.

    - o **Applications**: Lightweight structural components, engine parts, complex geometries.

6. **Consumer Goods**

    - o **Materials**: PLA, ABS, flexible filaments, photopolymer resins.

    - o **Applications**: Custom toys, household items, fashion accessories, electronics housings.

7. **Education and Research**

    - o **Materials**: PLA, standard resins, flexible filaments.

    - o **Applications**: Educational models, research prototypes, scientific instruments.

8. **Art and Fashion**

    - o **Materials**: Photopolymer resins, flexible filaments, metal-filled composites.

- o **Applications**: Sculptures, jewelry, avant-garde fashion pieces.

9. **Architecture and Construction**

    - o **Materials**: PLA, ABS, concrete-like materials.

    - o **Applications**: Scale models, architectural mockups, construction components.

10. **Food**

    - o **Materials**: Edible materials such as chocolate, sugar, and dough.

    - o **Applications**: Custom chocolates, intricate cake decorations, personalized food items.

Advantages of Using 3D – Print Materials

- **Customization**: Ability to create bespoke and intricate designs.

- **Complex Geometries**: Production of parts with complex shapes and internal structures.

- **Material Efficiency**: Reduced waste compared to traditional manufacturing.

- **Rapid Production**: Quick turnaround from design to final product.

Considerations When Choosing 3D – Print Materials

- **Mechanical Properties**: Strength, flexibility, and durability requirements of the part.

- **Thermal Properties**: Heat resistance needed for the application.

- **Surface Finish**: Desired smoothness and detail level.

- **Biocompatibility**: Suitability for medical and dental applications.

- **Cost**: Material cost relative to the project budget.

The selection of 3D printing materials is crucial to achieving the desired performance and quality of the printed parts, making it essential to understand the properties and applications of each material type.

Additive Manufacturing workflow

3D printing is only one step in the overall additive manufacturing workflow. For most AM production applications, the workflow will look something like this:

1. **Design the part.** Design may mean modifying an existing design for 3D printing, or starting from scratch with a true design for additive manufacturing (DFAM) mindset. Computer simulation, generative design and topology optimization can all be applied to optimize the function of the part. Printing process and material selection usually occurs in the initial design step.
2. **Plan the build.** Depending on the intended 3D printing technology, this step may entail selecting part orientation, adding support structures, packing or nesting multiple parts together, and setting printer parameters such as layer height, laser spot size, feed rate, etc.
3. **3D prints the part.** A 3D printing build might take anywhere from minutes to days.
4. **Post process the part.** Depending on the process, post processing could entail unpacking powder, prying or cutting parts from a build platform, cleaning, curing, heat treating, hot isostatic pressing (HIPping), etc.
5. **Finish the part.** Many 3D printed tools and production parts will require further finishing arriving at their completed state. Finishing steps might include machining surfaces, drilling or tapping holes, dyeing, coating or painting, and possibly welding or assembly with other parts.
6. **Inspect the part.** Some parts can be evaluated with CMM measurement or 3D scanning; those with complex internal features may require X-ray or CT scanning.

Different parts and applications may call for fewer or more steps. A hand tool made with fused filament fabrication (FFF) may not require any additional post processing once removed from the build plate. Parts with particularly stringent requirements, however, may require many more steps.

43

3. SKILLS TO START BUSINESSES

Starting an additive manufacturing (AM) business requires a combination of technical skills, business acumen, and industry knowledge.

Here are the essential technical skills needed to successfully launch and run an AM business:

Business Technology Stack:

1. 3D Modeling and CAD Skills

- **Software Proficiency**: Knowledge of CAD software such as AutoCAD, SolidWorks, Fusion 360, or Blender is essential for designing and modifying 3D models.

- **Design for Additive Manufacturing (DfAM)**: Understanding how to design parts that are optimized for 3D printing, including considerations for support structures, overhangs, and print orientation.

2. 3D Printing Technology Knowledge

- **Printer Operation**: Familiarity with different types of 3D printers (FDM, SLA, SLS, etc.) and their specific operating procedures.

- **Material Science**: Understanding the properties and applications of various 3D printing materials such as thermoplastics, resins, metals, and composites.

- **Post-Processing Techniques**: Knowledge of finishing processes like sanding, polishing, painting, and assembly to achieve the desired quality and appearance of printed parts.

3. Slicing Software Proficiency

- **Software Tools**: Ability to use slicing software (e.g., Cura, PrusaSlicer, PreForm) to prepare 3D models for printing, including setting print parameters, generating support structures, and optimizing print settings.

- **G-Code Understanding**: Basic understanding of G-code commands that control the printer's movements and functions.

4. Mechanical and Electrical Skills

- **Printer Maintenance**: Skills to troubleshoot and maintain 3D printers, including calibration, part replacement, and routine maintenance.

- **Assembly Skills**: Ability to assemble and disassemble printer components and handle repairs.

5. Quality Control and Assurance

- **Inspection Techniques**: Knowledge of methods to inspect printed parts for defects, accuracy, and adherence to specifications.

- **Quality Standards**: Familiarity with industry standards and certifications related to additive manufacturing (e.g., ISO/ASTM standards).

6. Prototyping and Product Development

- **Rapid Prototyping**: Skills to quickly iterate on designs and produce functional prototypes.

- **Product Testing**: Ability to test and validate prototypes to ensure they meet functional and performance requirements.

7. Project Management

- **Workflow Management**: Ability to manage the entire printing process from design to final product, ensuring efficient use of time and resources.

- **Client Communication**: Skills to communicate effectively with clients about project requirements, timelines, and deliverables.

8. Business and Financial Skills

- **Market Analysis**: Understanding market needs and identifying opportunities for additive manufacturing solutions.

- **Cost Estimation**: Ability to calculate costs related to materials, printing time, labor, and post-processing to price products and services competitively.

- **Supply Chain Management**: Knowledge of sourcing materials, managing inventory, and establishing relationships with suppliers.

9. Intellectual Property Management

- **IP Protection**: Understanding of how to protect intellectual property related to 3D designs and printed products, including patents, trademarks, and copyrights.

- **Compliance**: Ensuring compliance with legal and regulatory requirements in the industry.

10. Marketing and Sales

- **Digital Marketing**: Skills to promote the business through online channels, including social media, websites, and e-commerce platforms.

- **Sales Strategies**: Developing strategies to attract and retain customers, including direct sales, partnerships, and attending trade shows.

By combining these technical skills with business knowledge and continuous learning, you can successfully start and grow an additive manufacturing business.

Software Skills

Starting an additive manufacturing (AM) business requires proficiency in a variety of 3D modeling and printing software tools. Here are the key software skills you need to develop:

3D Modeling and CAD Software Skills

1. **CAD (Computer-Aided Design) Software Proficiency**

   o **AutoCAD**: Widely used for creating 2D and 3D designs. Essential for drafting and detailed design work.

   o **SolidWorks**: Powerful for creating complex models and assemblies, commonly used in engineering and product design.

   o **Fusion 360**: Offers cloud-based collaboration, integrates CAD, CAM, and CAE tools, suitable for product development and manufacturing.

   o **Blender**: Free and open-source, good for creating highly detailed and artistic 3D models, often used in animation and game design.

   o **TinkerCAD**: Beginner-friendly and web-based, suitable for basic modeling and educational purposes.

Skills:

- **Parametric Modeling**: Creating models based on parameters that can be easily modified.

- **Surface Modeling**: Designing complex surfaces and curves.

- **Solid Modeling**: Constructing 3D objects with volume.

- **Assembly Design**: Combining multiple parts into a single functional unit.

- **Rendering**: Creating visual representations of models for presentations and marketing.

2. Slicing Software Skills

- **Cura**: Free and open-source, developed by Ultimaker, supports many 3D printers.

- **PrusaSlicer**: Free, open-source, developed by Prusa Research, highly customizable.

- **Simplify3D**: Paid software with advanced features for optimizing print settings and supports.

- **PreForm**: Developed by Formlabs, used for preparing prints on their SLA printers.

Skills:

- **Layer Settings**: Adjusting layer height, infill density, and print speed.

- **Support Generation**: Creating supports for overhangs and complex geometries.

- **Print Orientation**: Optimizing the orientation of models to improve strength and reduce print time.

- **Material Settings**: Setting temperature, flow rate, and cooling for different materials.

- **Preview and Simulation**: Analyzing the print sequence and identifying potential issues before printing.

3. 3D Scanning and Mesh Editing Software Skills

- **MeshLab**: Free and open-source, used for processing and editing 3D meshes.

- **Geomagic Design X**: Advanced tool for converting 3D scan data into CAD models.

- **Blender**: Also useful for editing and refining scanned models.

Skills:

- **Mesh Cleaning**: Removing artifacts and fixing errors in scanned models.

- **Mesh Simplification**: Reducing the complexity of models while preserving essential features.

- **Retopology**: Creating a clean and optimized mesh from scan data.

- **Texture Mapping**: Applying textures to enhance the appearance of models.

4. Simulation and Analysis Software Skills

- **ANSYS**: Comprehensive tool for finite element analysis (FEA) and computational fluid dynamics (CFD).

- **SimScale**: Cloud-based simulation platform offering various analysis types.

- **Autodesk Nastran**: FEA tool integrated with Autodesk's CAD software.

Skills:

- **Structural Analysis**: Assessing the strength and durability of printed parts.

- **Thermal Analysis**: Understanding how parts will respond to temperature changes.

- **Flow Analysis**: Analyzing fluid flow within or around parts.

5. Post-Processing Software Skills

- **Magics by Materialise**: Advanced tool for preparing models for 3D printing, including support generation and part repair.

- **Netfabb by Autodesk**: Offers mesh repair, slicing, and build preparation features.

Skills:

- **File Repair**: Fixing issues with STL files to ensure successful printing.

- **Support Optimization**: Refining support structures to minimize material usage and improve surface quality.

- **Build Preparation**: Arranging parts on the build platform for optimal printing.

By mastering these software tools and skills, you can effectively design, prepare, and produce high-quality 3D printed parts, setting a strong foundation for your additive manufacturing business.

Hardware Skills

Starting an additive manufacturing (AM) business requires not only software proficiency but also a solid understanding of 3D modeling and printing hardware. Here are the essential hardware skills needed to successfully launch and operate an AM business:

3D Modeling Hardware Skills

1. **Computer Hardware Knowledge**

   - **High-Performance Computing**: Understanding the requirements for running resource-intensive CAD and 3D modeling software, including:

     - **Processor (CPU)**: Multi-core processors for faster computation.

- **Graphics Card (GPU)**: High-end GPUs for rendering and real-time visualization.

- **RAM**: Sufficient memory (16GB or more) for handling large files and complex models.

- **Storage**: SSDs for faster data access and large HDDs for storage of models and project files.

- **Peripheral Devices**: Familiarity with input devices such as 3D mice, digital drawing tablets, and high-resolution monitors for detailed design work.

3D Printing Hardware Skills

1. **3D Printer Operation and Maintenance**

   - **Types of 3D Printers**: Understanding the operational principles, strengths, and limitations of different types of 3D printers:

     - **FDM/FFF (Fused Deposition Modeling/Fused Filament Fabrication)**: Knowledge of filament handling, print bed leveling, and extrusion settings.

     - **SLA (Stereolithography)**: Handling of resin, cleaning, curing processes, and maintenance of laser systems.

     - **SLS (Selective Laser Sintering)**: Powder handling, post-processing of sintered parts, and maintenance of laser systems.

     - **DMLS/SLM (Direct Metal Laser Sintering/Selective Laser Melting)**: Metal powder management, inert gas environments, and high-power laser maintenance.

- o **Routine Maintenance**: Skills in cleaning, lubricating, calibrating, and replacing worn or damaged parts to ensure optimal printer performance.

- o **Troubleshooting**: Ability to diagnose and fix common printing issues such as nozzle clogs, layer shifting, warping, and adhesion problems.

2. **Printer Assembly and Upgrades**

- o **Assembly Skills**: Competence in assembling and disassembling 3D printers, understanding the mechanical and electrical components involved.

- o **Upgrading Components**: Knowledge of upgrading printer components such as hotends, extruders, build plates, and firmware to enhance performance and capabilities.

3. **Calibration and Optimization**

- o **Calibration Techniques**: Proficiency in calibrating various aspects of 3D printers, including:

    - **Build Plate Leveling**: Ensuring the print bed is level for consistent first-layer adhesion.

    - **Extruder Calibration**: Setting the correct extrusion multiplier and flow rate for accurate material deposition.

    - **Axis Calibration**: Ensuring the X, Y, and Z axes move accurately and smoothly.

- o **Print Optimization**: Fine-tuning print settings such as temperature, speed, and cooling to achieve the best print quality and reduce failures.

Post-Processing Hardware Skills

1. **Post-Processing Tools and Equipment**

   o **Finishing Tools**: Proficiency in using tools such as sanders, polishers, and dremels to smooth and finish printed parts.

   o **Cleaning Equipment**: Using ultrasonic cleaners, solvent baths, and air compressors to clean printed parts, especially for SLA and SLS prints.

   o **Curing Stations**: Knowledge of UV curing stations for post-processing resin prints to achieve full hardness and stability.

2. **Safety and Handling**

   o **Material Safety**: Understanding the safe handling and disposal of various 3D printing materials, including resins, powders, and filaments.

   o **Personal Protective Equipment (PPE)**: Using appropriate PPE such as gloves, masks, and safety goggles to protect against hazardous materials and fumes.

   o **Work Environment**: Setting up a safe and organized workspace, ensuring proper ventilation and storage for 3D printing materials.

General Technical Skills

1. **Electrical and Mechanical Skills**

   o **Basic Electronics**: Understanding basic electronics, including wiring, soldering, and circuit troubleshooting, especially for printer maintenance and custom modifications.

- o **Mechanical Assembly**: Skills in assembling and maintaining mechanical systems, such as stepper motors, linear rails, and bearings used in 3D printers.

2. **Networking and IT Skills**

- o **Network Setup**: Setting up and managing a network of 3D printers, including Wi-Fi or Ethernet connections for remote monitoring and control.

- o **Firmware Updates**: Installing and updating printer firmware to ensure compatibility with new features and improvements.

By developing these hardware skills, you can ensure the efficient operation and maintenance of your 3D printers, ultimately contributing to the success of your additive manufacturing business.

Maintenance and Troubleshooting

Starting an additive manufacturing (AM) business involves not only understanding the technology but also ensuring the longevity and efficiency of your equipment. This requires knowledge of 3D printer maintenance, troubleshooting, material and waste management, and having the right toolset. Here's a comprehensive guide to these aspects:

1. 3D Printer Maintenance

Routine Maintenance

- **Cleaning**: Regularly clean the print bed, nozzle, and other components to prevent buildup of debris and material residues.

- **Lubrication**: Lubricate moving parts such as rails, lead screws, and bearings to ensure smooth operation.

- **Calibration**: Frequently calibrate the printer's axes and bed leveling to maintain print accuracy.

- **Firmware Updates**: Keep the printer's firmware up to date to benefit from the latest features and improvements.

- **Filter Replacement**: For printers with air filtration systems, replace filters as recommended by the manufacturer.

Periodic Maintenance

- **Nozzle Replacement**: Replace worn or clogged nozzles to maintain print quality.

- **Belt Tension**: Check and adjust the tension of belts to avoid skipping and ensure precise movements.

- **Extruder Inspection**: Inspect and clean the extruder mechanism to prevent jams and ensure consistent filament feeding.

- **Heat Bed Inspection**: Check the heat bed for even heating and replace any faulty components.

2. Troubleshooting Common Issues

Print Quality Problems

- **Layer Shifting**: Ensure belts are tight and pulleys are secure. Check for obstructions in the printer's path.

- **Warping**: Use a heated bed, apply adhesives like glue stick or painter's tape, and adjust bed temperature.

- **Stringing**: Adjust retraction settings and print temperature to minimize stringing.

- **Under-Extrusion**: Check for clogs in the nozzle, ensure filament is feeding properly, and adjust extrusion multiplier.

- **Over-Extrusion**: Reduce the extrusion multiplier or flow rate.

Mechanical Issues

- **Motor Malfunctions**: Check connections and ensure stepper drivers are functioning correctly.

- **Bed Leveling Issues**: Recalibrate the bed manually or use an automatic leveling system.

- **Z-Axis Wobble**: Ensure the Z-axis is properly aligned and that lead screws are straight and secure.

Electrical Issues

- **Sensor Failures**: Replace faulty sensors such as thermistors or endstops.

- **Heating Issues**: Inspect and replace heating elements or thermistors if the bed or nozzle fails to reach the desired temperature.

- **Connection Problems**: Check and secure all wiring connections.

3. Material and Waste Management

Material Storage

- **Filament Storage**: Store filaments in airtight containers with desiccants to prevent moisture absorption.

- **Resin Storage**: Keep resin in opaque containers to protect it from light and store at recommended temperatures.

- **Powder Storage**: Store powder materials in dry conditions to prevent clumping and contamination.

Waste Management

- **Material Recycling**: Implement recycling programs for used filaments and supports. Some manufacturers offer recycling services.

- **Resin Disposal**: Dispose of resin waste according to local regulations. Use UV light to cure liquid resin waste before disposal.

- **Powder Handling**: Use proper PPE (personal protective equipment) to handle powders and dispose of unused powder safely.

- **Print Waste Reduction**: Optimize print settings to minimize support structures and material wastage. Use software to nest parts efficiently.

4. Essential Toolset for Maintenance and Troubleshooting

Basic Tools

- **Allen Wrenches/Hex Keys**: For assembling and adjusting printer components.

- **Screwdrivers**: Phillips and flathead screwdrivers for various fasteners.

- **Pliers and Tweezers**: For handling small parts and filament removal.

- **Cutters and Snips**: For cutting filament and trimming printed parts.

- **Digital Calipers**: For precise measurements and ensuring dimensional accuracy of printed parts.

- **Spatulas/Scrapers**: For removing prints from the build plate.

Specialized Tools

- **Nozzle Cleaning Kit**: For unclogging nozzles and maintaining extrusion quality.

- **Multimeter**: For diagnosing electrical issues.

- **Thermocouple**: For verifying the temperature of the nozzle and heat bed.

- **Lubricants**: High-quality lubricants for maintaining smooth operation of moving parts.

- **Belt Tension Gauge**: For checking and adjusting belt tension accurately.

Safety Equipment

- **Safety Glasses**: To protect eyes from debris and resin splashes.

- **Gloves**: For handling hot components and chemicals.

- **Respirators/Masks**: To protect against fumes and fine particles, especially when working with resins and powders.

Learning Resources

1. **Manufacturer Manuals and Guides**: Always refer to the printer's official documentation for maintenance and troubleshooting procedures.

2. **Online Tutorials and Forums**: Websites like Reddit's r/3Dprinting, forums, and YouTube channels offer community support and tutorials.

3. **Workshops and Training Programs**: Participate in workshops and training sessions offered by printer manufacturers or industry organizations.

4. **Technical Support Services**: Utilize technical support from printer manufacturers for complex issues.

Maintaining and troubleshooting 3D printers, managing materials and waste, and having the right toolset are crucial aspects of running a successful additive manufacturing business. Mastery of these skills ensures consistent print quality, efficient operations, and compliance with safety and environmental regulations. By staying informed and equipped, you can effectively manage your AM business and deliver high-quality products to your clients.

4. MODELING SOFTWARE

To start an additive manufacturing (AM) business, proficiency in 3D modeling software is crucial. These tools are used to create and modify digital 3D models that can be printed using various 3D printing technologies. Here's a comprehensive guide to some of the most popular and useful 3D modeling software options, their features, and applications in an AM business:

1. AutoCAD

Overview: AutoCAD is one of the most widely used CAD (Computer-Aided Design) software applications, known for its robust set of features and versatility.

Key Features:

- **2D and 3D Design**: Capabilities for creating both detailed 2D drawings and complex 3D models.

- **Precision and Control**: Tools for precise measurements and detailed design modifications.

- **Compatibility**: Supports a wide range of file formats, making it easy to integrate with other software.

Applications:

- Architectural design, mechanical engineering, and product development.

2. SolidWorks

Overview: SolidWorks is a powerful CAD software specifically tailored for mechanical design and product development.

Key Features:

- **Parametric Design**: Allows you to design parts and assemblies with relationships and constraints that ensure accuracy.

- **Simulation**: Integrated simulation tools to test and validate designs under real-world conditions.

- **Collaboration**: Cloud-based collaboration tools for team-based projects.

Applications:

- Mechanical engineering, industrial design, and complex product assemblies.

3. Fusion 360

Overview: Fusion 360 by Autodesk is a cloud-based CAD/CAM/CAE tool that combines industrial and mechanical design, simulation, collaboration, and machining.

Key Features:

- **Integrated Workflow**: Combines CAD, CAM, and CAE tools in one platform.

- **Collaboration**: Cloud-based features enable real-time collaboration and access to designs from anywhere.

- **Simulation and Analysis**: Tools for simulating mechanical stresses and analyzing product performance.

Applications:

- Product design, mechanical engineering, and manufacturing.

4. Blender

Overview: Blender is a free and open-source 3D modeling software known for its versatility in modeling, animation, and rendering.

Key Features:

- **Modeling and Sculpting**: Advanced tools for creating highly detailed models.

- **Animation and Rigging**: Capabilities for creating animations and character rigging.

- **Rendering**: High-quality rendering engine for creating realistic images and animations.

Applications:

- Animation, game design, and creating artistic or highly detailed models.

5. TinkerCAD

Overview: TinkerCAD is an easy-to-use, web-based 3D modeling and CAD tool that is particularly suitable for beginners.

Key Features:

- **User-Friendly Interface**: Simple and intuitive interface for quick learning.

- **Shape Library**: Extensive library of pre-designed shapes and objects.

- **Integration**: Easily integrates with 3D printing workflows.

Applications:

- Educational purposes, hobbyist projects, and simple design tasks.

6. Rhino (Rhinoceros)

Overview: Rhino is a 3D modeling software known for its ability to handle complex surfaces and organic shapes.

Key Features:

- **NURBS Modeling**: Uses NURBS (Non-Uniform Rational B-Splines) for creating accurate and flexible 3D models.

- **Plugins and Scripting**: Extensive plugin support and scripting capabilities for customized workflows.

- **Precision**: High level of precision in creating and editing models.

Applications:

- Industrial design, jewelry design, and architectural visualization.

7. Onshape

Overview: Onshape is a cloud-based CAD platform that offers powerful modeling tools and collaboration features.

Key Features:

- **Cloud-Based**: Access and collaborate on designs from any device with internet connectivity.

- **Version Control**: Built-in version control to manage design iterations.

- **Collaboration**: Real-time collaboration tools for team-based projects.

Applications:

- Mechanical engineering, product design, and team-based design projects.

8. SketchUp

Overview: SketchUp is a user-friendly 3D modeling software that is particularly popular in architecture and construction.

Key Features:

- **Ease of Use**: Intuitive interface that allows for quick learning and fast modeling.

- **Extensive Library**: Access to a large library of pre-made models and components.

- **Plugins**: Wide range of plugins to extend functionality.

Applications:

- Architectural design, interior design, and landscape architecture.

Learning Resources and Support

1. **Online Courses and Tutorials**

    o **Coursera, Udemy, LinkedIn Learning**: Offer courses on specific software tools and general 3D modeling skills.

    o **YouTube**: Numerous channels dedicated to tutorials and tips for different 3D modeling software.

2. **Books and Manuals**

    o **Software Manuals**: Official manuals and user guides from software developers.

    o **Specialized Books**: Books focused on specific software or aspects of 3D modeling and design.

3. **Community and Forums**

    o **Online Communities**: Platforms like Reddit, Stack Exchange, and specific software forums for peer support and knowledge sharing.

    o **User Groups**: Local or online user groups for networking and collaborative learning.

Choosing the right 3D modeling software depends on the specific needs of your additive manufacturing business, such as the types of products you plan to design and the level of complexity required. Investing time in learning and mastering these tools will enable you to create high-quality 3D models, optimize designs for printing, and ultimately deliver superior products to your clients.

3D – Modeling using Blender

Blender is versatile and powerful open-source 3D modeling software widely used for creating detailed models, animations, visual effects, and more. It's especially popular among artists, animators, game developers, and designers due to its robust feature set and flexibility. Here's a detailed overview of Blender's capabilities and its application in 3D modeling and printing:

Overview of Blender

Blender is known for its:

- **Open-Source Nature**: Blender is free to use and its source code is freely available, allowing for customization and community-driven development.

- **Cross-Platform Compatibility**: It runs on Windows, macOS, and Linux, making it accessible to a wide range of users.

- **Comprehensive Toolset**: Blender includes a full suite of tools for modeling, sculpting, texturing, rigging, animation, rendering, compositing, and video editing.

Key Features of Blender for 3D Modeling and Printing

1. **Modeling Tools**

   - **Mesh Modeling**: Blender offers a variety of tools for creating and editing polygonal meshes, including extrusion, beveling, boolean operations, and more.

   - **Sculpting**: Detailed sculpting tools for creating organic shapes and high-resolution details.

   - **Modifiers**: A wide range of modifiers to non-destructively alter geometry, such as mirror, array, and subdivision surface modifiers.

2. **UV Mapping and Texturing**

- o **UV Editing**: Tools for unwrapping 3D models and efficiently laying out UV maps for texturing.

- o **Texture Painting**: Integrated painting tools for creating and editing textures directly on 3D models.

3. **Animation and Rigging**

- o **Armature System**: Tools for creating skeletal rigs and animating characters and objects.

- o **Keyframe Animation**: Keyframe-based animation system for animating objects, cameras, and lights.

- o **Physics Simulation**: Built-in physics simulation engines for realistic animations, including cloth, fluid, and particles.

4. **Rendering and Visualization**

- o **Cycles Renderer**: Blender's powerful path-tracing renderer for producing photorealistic images and animations.

- o **Eevee Renderer**: Real-time render engine for interactive previews and fast rendering of animations.

- o **Viewport Shading**: Various shading modes for previewing materials and textures directly in the viewport.

5. **Add-ons and Customization**

- o **Scripting and Automation**: Python scripting support for automating tasks and extending Blender's functionality.

- o **Add-on System**: Extensive library of add-ons contributed by the community, enhancing Blender's capabilities for specific tasks.

6. **Integration with 3D Printing Workflows**

    o   **STL Support**: Blender can import and export STL files, the standard format used for 3D printing.

    o   **Mesh Analysis Tools**: Tools for checking and repairing meshes to ensure they are manifold and suitable for 3D printing.

    o   **Printing Orientation**: Ability to optimize the orientation of models for 3D printing to minimize supports and achieve better print quality.

Applications of Blender in Additive Manufacturing

1. **Prototyping and Product Design**

    o   Blender is used to create detailed prototypes and product designs, optimizing shapes and structures for functional testing and visualization.

2. **Customization and Personalization**

    o   It allows for the customization of products based on specific user requirements or client preferences, enhancing the flexibility of additive manufacturing services.

3. **Artistic and Creative Applications**

    o   Artists and designers use Blender to create artistic and visually appealing models that can be 3D printed, ranging from sculptures to intricate designs.

Learning and Resources

1. **Tutorials and Documentation**

    o   **Blender.org**: Official documentation and tutorials provided by the Blender Foundation.

o **YouTube**: Many channels offer tutorials on Blender's various features and workflows for beginners to advanced users.

2. **Community Support**

   o **Blender Artists**: A popular online community where users can share artwork, ask questions, and get feedback.

   o **Blender Stack Exchange**: Q&A site for technical questions and troubleshooting.

3. **Books and Courses**

   o Various books and online courses are available through platforms like Udemy, Coursera, and LinkedIn Learning, covering Blender's use in 3D modeling and printing.

Blender's versatility, powerful feature set, and community support make it an excellent choice for 3D modeling and printing in additive manufacturing. Whether you're creating prototypes, customized products, or artistic designs, Blender provides the tools and flexibility needed to bring your ideas to life and prepare them for 3D printing with precision and efficiency.

Working Procedure:

Working with Blender for 3D modeling involves mastering its interface, understanding basic modeling techniques, and utilizing its wide array of tools for creating detailed and complex models. Here's a comprehensive guide to get you started with Blender for 3D modeling:

Getting Started with Blender

1. **Download and Installation**

   o Visit the Blender website (https://www.blender.org/) and download the latest version of Blender for your operating system (Windows, macOS, Linux).

o   Install Blender following the on-screen instructions.

2. **Navigating the Blender Interface**

   o   **Viewport**: The main 3D view where you interact with your models.

   o   **Tool Shelf and Properties Panel**: Panels on the left and right sides of the viewport containing tools, settings, and properties.

   o   **Header**: Toolbar at the top with menus and options for different modes and operations.

3. **Basic Navigation**

   o   **Rotate**: Middle mouse button (MMB) + move mouse.

   o   **Pan**: Shift + MMB + move mouse.

   o   **Zoom**: Scroll wheel or Ctrl + MMB + move mouse.

4. **Creating and Editing Objects**

   o   **Adding Objects**: Press Shift + A or use the Add menu (Add > Mesh) to add basic objects like cubes, spheres, cylinders, etc.

   o   **Editing Mode**: Switch to Edit Mode (Tab key) to manipulate the vertices, edges, and faces of objects.

   o   **Vertex, Edge, Face Selection**: Select vertices (1), edges (2), or faces (3) to perform operations on specific parts of the mesh.

5. **Modeling Techniques**

   o   **Extrusion**: Select a face or edge and press E to extrude (create new geometry from existing).

- **Loop Cut and Slide**: Ctrl + R to add loop cuts for creating edge loops that refine the shape of the mesh.

- **Bevel**: Ctrl + B to bevel edges (create rounded edges).

- **Boolean Operations**: Use Boolean modifiers (Add Modifier > Boolean) to combine or subtract objects.

6. **Modifiers**

- **Mirror**: Mirror modifier (Add Modifier > Mirror) for symmetrical modeling.

- **Subdivision Surface**: Subdivide geometry to create smoother surfaces (Add Modifier > Subdivision Surface).

7. **Texturing and UV Mapping**

- **UV Editing**: Switch to UV Editing workspace for unwrapping the mesh and applying textures (select faces, U > Unwrap).

- **Materials**: Create and assign materials to objects using the Node Editor (Shader Editor) to control surface appearance.

8. **Rendering**

- **Cycles Renderer**: Set up materials, lighting, and camera, then render high-quality images with the Cycles render engine.

- **Eevee Renderer**: Real-time rendering for quick previews and animations.

9. **Animation and Rigging**

- **Armature**: Use armatures and bones (Add > Armature) to rig models for animation.

o **Keyframes**: Set keyframes to animate object properties (location, rotation, scale) and characters.

10. **Exporting for 3D Printing**

   o **File Formats**: Export models as STL or OBJ files (File > Export > STL/OBJ) for compatibility with 3D printing software.

Learning Resources

- **Blender Documentation**: Official guides and manuals available on the Blender website.

- **YouTube Tutorials**: Many tutorial channels offer step-by-step guides and project-based learning for Blender.

- **Blender Artists Community**: Online forums and communities for sharing work, asking questions, and getting feedback.

Tips for Success

- **Practice Regularly**: Experiment with different tools and techniques to become comfortable with Blender's interface and workflow.

- **Start with Simple Projects**: Begin with basic modeling exercises and gradually tackle more complex projects as you gain confidence.

- **Utilize Keyboard Shortcuts**: Blender has extensive keyboard shortcuts that can significantly speed up your workflow once mastered.

By following these steps and utilizing the resources available, you can effectively learn Blender for 3D modeling and begin creating detailed models for various applications, including animation, visual effects, game development, and 3D prints.

3D – Modeling using Tinkercad

Tinkercad is a user-friendly, web-based 3D modeling software developed by Autodesk. It is designed to introduce beginners to 3D modeling and is widely used in educational settings and by hobbyists. Here's an overview of Tinkercad and its applications in 3D modeling and printing businesses:

Overview of Tinkercad

1. **Accessibility and Interface**

   - **Web-Based**: Tinkercad runs entirely in a web browser, eliminating the need for software installation and making it accessible from any device with internet access.

   - **User-Friendly**: Designed with a simple and intuitive interface, Tinkercad is easy to learn and suitable for users with no prior experience in 3D modeling.

2. **Key Features**

   - **Shape Generators**: Provides a variety of basic shapes and pre-designed objects that users can easily drag and drop to create models.

   - **Solid Modeling**: Uses constructive solid geometry (CSG) techniques, allowing users to combine primitive shapes (like cubes, cylinders, and spheres) to create more complex forms.

   - **Workplane**: Allows users to place objects on a virtual workplane and manipulate them in 3D space.

   - **Alignment and Measurement Tools**: Tools for aligning objects precisely and measuring dimensions.

3. **Integration with 3D Printing**

   o **STL Export**: Tinkercad allows users to export models in STL (Standard Tessellation Language) format, which is compatible with most 3D printers.

   o **Printing Preparation**: While basic, Tinkercad provides tools for adjusting the size and orientation of models to optimize them for 3D printing.

Applications in 3D Modeling and Printing Business

1. **Educational Use**

   o **Introduction to 3D Modeling**: Tinkercad is often used in classrooms to teach students the fundamentals of 3D design and printing.

   o **Prototyping**: It can be used for creating simple prototypes and mock-ups quickly.

2. **Hobbyist and Maker Projects**

   o **DIY Projects**: Tinkercad is popular among hobbyists and makers for creating custom designs for personal projects, such as accessories, toys, and decorative items.

3. **Design Iterations and Conceptualization**

   o **Rapid Prototyping**: Allows for quick iteration and visualization of design concepts before committing to more complex modeling software or production.

Learning and Resources

1. **Tutorials and Documentation**

   o **Autodesk Tinkercad Website**: Provides tutorials and resources for learning Tinkercad, including step-by-step guides and video tutorials.

- o **YouTube**: Many tutorial channels offer guides on using Tinkercad for various projects and applications.

2. **Community Support**

   - o **Tinkercad Community**: Users can share designs, ask questions, and get feedback from other Tinkercad users in the online community.

3. **Educational Resources**

   - o **Lesson Plans**: Autodesk provides educators with curriculum materials and lesson plans for incorporating Tinkercad into classroom activities.

Tinkercad's simplicity and accessibility make it an excellent tool for beginners and educators looking to explore 3D modeling and printing. While it may lack some of the advanced features found in professional CAD software, its ease of use and integration with 3D printing make it suitable for prototyping, educational purposes, and quick design iterations in 3D printing businesses. For more complex designs and advanced features, users may eventually transition to more powerful CAD software like Autodesk Fusion 360 or SolidWorks as their skills and needs grow.

Working Procedure:

Working with Tinkercad for 3D modeling is straightforward and designed to be user-friendly, making it accessible even for beginners. Here's a step-by-step guide to help you get started with Tinkercad:

Getting Started with Tinkercad

1. **Create an Account and Log In**

   - o Visit the Tinkercad website (www.tinkercad.com) and sign up for a free account if you haven't already.

   - o Log in to your account to access the Tinkercad workspace.

2. **Explore the Tinkercad Interface**

   o Upon logging in, you'll see the Tinkercad workspace, which consists of several panels and tools:

      ▪ **Dashboard**: Where you can access your projects and create new ones.

      ▪ **Workplane**: The main area where you'll create and manipulate your 3D models.

      ▪ **Shape Generators**: Basic shapes and objects that you can drag and drop onto the workplane to start creating.

      ▪ **Design Tools**: Tools for moving, rotating, scaling, and aligning objects.

3. **Creating Your First Model**

   o **Add Basic Shapes**:

      ▪ Start by dragging a basic shape (e.g., cube, cylinder, sphere) from the Shape Generators panel onto the workplane.

      ▪ You can adjust the size and dimensions of the shape using the handles that appear when you select it.

   o **Manipulate Objects**:

      ▪ Use the arrow handles to move objects in different directions.

      ▪ Rotate objects using the circular handles that appear around the object.

      ▪ Scale objects by dragging the corner handles to resize them proportionally.

- **Combine Shapes**:

    - Create more complex shapes by combining basic shapes using Boolean operations (Union, Difference, Intersection):

        - **Union**: Joins two or more shapes together.

        - **Difference**: Removes one shape from another.

        - **Intersection**: Creates a new shape where two shapes overlap.

- **Group and Ungroup Objects**:

    - Select multiple objects and group them together to treat them as a single object.

    - Ungroup objects to edit individual components separately.

4. **Editing and Customizing**

- **Shape Editing**:

    - Double-click on a shape to enter edit mode where you can manipulate its vertices, edges, and faces to create custom shapes.

    - Use the shape adjustment handles to fine-tune the shape.

- **Adding Text and Custom Shapes**:

    - Use the Text tool to add 3D text to your model, adjusting the font, size, and depth.

    - Import custom shapes or SVG files to incorporate external designs into your project.

5. **Working with Measurements and Alignment**

   o **Snap Grid and Measurements**:

      - Enable the snap grid for precise alignment of objects on the workplane.

      - Use the ruler tool to measure distances between objects and ensure accurate dimensions.

6. **Preparing for 3D Printing**

   o **Checking Model Integrity**:

      - Use the solid inspector tool to check and repair your model for any issues that may affect 3D printing, such as non-manifold geometry.

   o **Exporting STL Files**:

      - Once your model is complete, export it as an STL file (File > Export > Download for 3D Printing).

      - STL files are widely accepted by 3D printing software and services.

7. **Additional Tools and Features**

   o **Circuit Design**: Tinkercad also offers tools for creating simple electronic circuits and integrating them into your 3D designs, useful for prototyping electronic projects.

Learning Resources

- **Tinkercad Lessons**: Explore the lessons and tutorials provided within the Tinkercad interface to learn specific skills and techniques.

- **YouTube Tutorials**: Many tutorial channels offer step-by-step guides and project ideas for using Tinkercad.

- **Community Support**: Join the Tinkercad community to share your work, ask questions, and learn from others.

Tips for Success

- **Start Simple**: Begin with basic shapes and gradually experiment with more complex designs and features.

- **Explore Shape Generators**: Utilize the pre-designed shape generators to speed up your workflow and explore different design possibilities.

- **Save Regularly**: Tinkercad auto-saves your work, but it's good practice to save versions of your designs as you progress.

By following these steps and exploring the tools and features of Tinkercad, you can create 3D models suitable for 3D printing and explore the creative possibilities of additive manufacturing.

3D – Modeling using Fusion 360:

Fusion 360 is a comprehensive CAD/CAM/CAE tool developed by Autodesk, specifically designed for product design, engineering, and manufacturing. It combines industrial and mechanical design, simulation, collaboration, and machining in a single platform. Here's an overview of Fusion 360 and its application in 3D modeling and printing businesses:

Key Features of Fusion 360

1. **Integrated CAD, CAM, and CAE**
   - **CAD (Computer-Aided Design)**:
     - **Parametric Modeling**: Fusion 360 uses parametric modeling techniques, allowing you to create models with design intent, where changes to dimensions and parameters update the entire model.

- **Freeform Modeling**: Tools for creating organic shapes and surfaces, useful for ergonomic designs and artistic models.
    - **Assembly Modeling**: Ability to create assemblies of multiple components, with constraints and relationships to simulate real-world motion.
  - **CAM (Computer-Aided Manufacturing)**:
    - **Toolpath Generation**: Generate toolpaths for CNC machining directly from your 3D models.
    - **Simulation and Verification**: Simulate machining operations to detect errors and optimize toolpaths for efficiency and quality.
  - **CAE (Computer-Aided Engineering)**:
    - **Simulation**: Perform stress analysis, thermal analysis, and modal analysis to test the performance and durability of designs under various conditions.
    - **Fluid Dynamics**: Analyze fluid flow and heat transfer for designs involving fluid systems.

2. **Cloud-Based Collaboration**
   - Fusion 360 is cloud-based, enabling real-time collaboration and version control. Team members can work on the same project simultaneously from different locations.

3. **Parametric Design and History**
   - o Fusion 360's parametric design approach allows you to capture design intent and make changes easily by updating parameters.
   - o History-based modeling tracks all design steps, facilitating design iteration and modification.

4. **Rendering and Visualization**
   - o High-quality rendering capabilities for creating realistic images and presentations of your designs.
   - o Visualize materials, textures, and lighting to communicate design concepts effectively.

5. **Additive Manufacturing and 3D Printing**
   - o Fusion 360 supports 3D printing workflows, allowing you to prepare models for additive manufacturing processes:
     - **Mesh Analysis**: Ensure models are watertight and suitable for 3D printing by analyzing mesh integrity.
     - **Slicing and G-Code Generation**: Prepare models for printing by generating G-code or exporting to STL format.
     - **Orientation and Support Structures**: Optimize print orientation and generate support structures to improve print quality.

6. **Electronics and PCB Design**
   - o Fusion 360 includes tools for designing electronic circuits and printed circuit boards (PCBs), integrating mechanical and electrical design workflows.

Applications in 3D Modeling and Printing Business

1. **Product Design and Prototyping**
   - Fusion 360 is ideal for designing prototypes and products across various industries, from consumer goods to industrial machinery.
   - Rapid prototyping capabilities allow for quick iteration and testing of design concepts.

2. **Mechanical Engineering**
   - Used in mechanical engineering for designing machine components, assemblies, and mechanisms.
   - Simulation tools help validate designs for performance and durability.

3. **Customization and Personalization**
   - Supports customization of products based on client requirements or market demands.
   - Easily adapt designs for different sizes, materials, and functionalities.

4. **Educational and Training Purposes**
   - Fusion 360 is used in educational settings to teach CAD/CAM principles and prepare students for careers in engineering and manufacturing.

Learning Resources

- **Autodesk Fusion 360 Website**: Offers tutorials, documentation, and community forums.
- **YouTube Tutorials**: Many channels provide step-by-step guides and project-based learning for Fusion 360.
- **Online Courses**: Available on platforms like Coursera, Udemy, and LinkedIn Learning.

Fusion 360's integration of CAD, CAM, and CAE functionalities, coupled with its cloud-based collaboration and simulation capabilities, makes it a powerful tool for 3D modeling and printing businesses. Whether you're designing products for manufacturing, optimizing designs for 3D printing, or simulating performance under various conditions, Fusion 360 provides the tools and flexibility needed to streamline your workflow and achieve high-quality results.

Working Procedure:

Working with Fusion 360 for 3D modeling and printing involves mastering its various tools and workflows, which are designed to support both design iteration and preparation for additive manufacturing processes. Here's a step-by-step guide to get you started with Fusion 360:

Getting Started with Fusion 360

1. **Download and Installation**
   - Visit the Autodesk Fusion 360 website (https://www.autodesk.com/products/fusion-360/overview) and download the software.
   - Install Fusion 360 following the on-screen instructions. You will need to sign in with your Autodesk account or create a new one.

2. **Navigating the Interface**
   - **Workspace**: Fusion 360 has different workspaces tailored to specific tasks (e.g., Design, Render, CAM, Simulation). Start with the Design workspace for 3D modeling.
   - **Toolbar**: Contains tools and commands for creating, modifying, and analyzing your models.

- o **Browser**: Displays the components, sketches, and other elements of your project.
- o **Canvas**: The main area where you create and manipulate your 3D models.

3. **Creating and Editing 3D Models**
   - o **Sketching**: Start by creating 2D sketches on planes (e.g., Top, Front, Right) using sketch tools (line, circle, arc, etc.).
     - Use dimensions and constraints to define the size and relationships between sketch entities.
   - o **Extrude and Revolve**: Turn 2D sketches into 3D shapes using the Extrude or Revolve commands.
     - Select a sketch, then use the Extrude command (E key) to pull the sketch into a 3D form.
     - Revolve (Create > Revolve) allows you to create a solid by rotating a profile around an axis.
   - o **Modeling Tools**: Fusion 360 offers a wide range of modeling tools, including:
     - **Fillet and Chamfer**: Rounds or bevels edges to create smoother transitions.
     - **Shell**: Hollows out a solid model to create thin-walled structures.
     - **Pattern**: Replicates features, bodies, or components in a linear, circular, or rectangular pattern.
   - o **Assemblies**: Combine multiple components into assemblies using joints and motion constraints to simulate mechanical assemblies.

4. **Preparing for 3D Printing**

   o **Mesh Analysis**: Ensure your model is suitable for 3D printing by checking for issues like non-manifold geometry or gaps using the Inspect tool (Inspect > Mesh > Analyze).

   o **Orientation and Supports**: Optimize the orientation of your model on the print bed to minimize supports and achieve better print quality.

   o **Exporting STL Files**: Once your model is ready, export it as an STL file (File > Export > STL) or other compatible formats for 3D printing.

5. **Simulation and Analysis**

   o Fusion 360 includes simulation tools for testing the performance and behavior of your designs under different conditions:

      - **Static Stress Analysis**: Analyzes how forces affect the structural integrity of your model.

      - **Thermal Analysis**: Simulates heat transfer and temperature distribution within your design.

      - **Modal Analysis**: Identifies natural frequencies and potential modes of vibration in your model.

6. **CAM (Computer-Aided Manufacturing)**

   o Fusion 360 integrates CAM tools for generating toolpaths and preparing designs for CNC machining:

      - **Toolpath Generation**: Define cutting operations, tools, and strategies for machining operations.

- **Simulation**: Verify toolpaths and simulate machining operations to detect errors and optimize performance.

Learning Resources

- **Autodesk Fusion 360 Help**: Access comprehensive documentation and tutorials directly within the software.
- **Autodesk University**: Offers online courses and learning paths for Fusion 360.
- **YouTube Tutorials**: Many tutorial channels provide step-by-step guides and project-based learning for Fusion 360.

Tips for Success

- **Start with Tutorials**: Begin with basic tutorials to familiarize yourself with Fusion 360's interface and fundamental tools.
- **Practice Regularly**: Experiment with different tools and workflows to build confidence and proficiency.
- **Join the Community**: Participate in forums and user groups to share experiences, ask questions, and learn from others.

By following these steps and utilizing the resources available, you can effectively use Fusion 360 for 3D modeling and printing, whether you're creating prototypes, optimizing designs for manufacturing, or preparing models for additive manufacturing processes.

Practice Exercises:

Practicing 3D modeling is essential to build skills and proficiency, whether you're using software like Blender, Fusion 360, Tinkercad, or any other CAD tool. Here are some practice exercises categorized by difficulty level:

Beginner Exercises

1. **Basic Shapes and Objects**

    o   Create simple geometric shapes: cube, sphere, cylinder, cone, pyramid.

    o   Combine basic shapes to create more complex forms (e.g., a house, a car, a table).

2. **Modeling from Reference Images**

    o   Find reference images (e.g., furniture, household items) and recreate them in 3D.

    o   Practice using basic modeling tools like extrusion, scaling, and rotation.

3. **Architectural Elements**

    o   Model basic architectural elements such as doors, windows, columns, and stairs.

    o   Combine these elements to create a simple building or structure.

4. **Character Modeling**

    o   Start with basic humanoid or animal characters.

    o   Focus on creating simple shapes and understanding anatomy proportions.

Intermediate Exercises

5. **Product Design**

    o   Choose a product (e.g., a phone, a watch, a kitchen appliance) and model it in detail.

    o   Pay attention to surface details, buttons, and functional components.

6. **Mechanical Parts**

    o   Model mechanical components like gears, nuts, bolts, and hinges.

    o   Practice using constraints and assembly techniques (if your software supports it).

7. **Organic Modeling**

    o   Create organic shapes such as fruits, plants, or animals with more complexity.

    o   Experiment with sculpting tools if available (e.g., in Blender).

8. **Environment Modeling**

    o   Model a scene with natural elements like trees, rocks, and terrain.

    o   Incorporate lighting and textures to create a realistic environment.

Advanced Exercises

9. **Vehicle Modeling**

    o   Model a vehicle of your choice (car, airplane, spaceship) with detailed interiors and exteriors.

    o   Include mechanical components like engines, seats, and controls.

10. **Complex Objects**

    o   Challenge yourself with intricate objects such as a detailed robot, a complex machinery assembly, or a cityscape.

- Focus on refining details, optimizing geometry, and ensuring functional realism.

11. **Character Animation**

  - Learn rigging and animation by creating a basic rig for a character (e.g., humanoid) and animating simple movements like walking or jumping.

  - Explore facial expressions and more complex animations as you progress.

12. **Simulation and Analysis**

  - Use simulation tools to analyze the structural integrity of a model under different stress conditions.

  - Experiment with thermal analysis to understand heat distribution in a design.

General Tips

- **Set Goals**: Define specific objectives for each exercise to focus your learning.

- **Iterate and Refine**: Don't be afraid to iterate on your designs to improve them.

- **Seek Feedback**: Share your work with others, join online communities, and ask for constructive feedback to improve your skills.

- **Explore Tutorials**: Follow tutorials and guides to learn new techniques and workflows.

By practicing these exercises regularly, you'll develop a solid foundation in 3D modeling, improve your technical skills, and gain confidence in using your chosen CAD software effectively.

5. SLICING AND PRINTER CONFIGURATIONS

Starting an additive manufacturing business involves understanding the critical aspects of 3D printing, including slicing software and printer configurations. Here's a detailed overview:

3D – Print Slicing Software

Slicing software is a tool that converts 3D models (usually in STL, OBJ, or 3MF format) into instructions (G-code) that a 3D printer can understand and execute.

Functions of Slicing Software:

1. **Model Preparation:** Importing and adjusting the 3D model (scaling, rotating, and positioning).

2. **Layer Slicing:** Dividing the model into horizontal layers that the printer will build one at a time.

3. **Setting Parameters:** Configuring print settings such as layer height, infill density, print speed, temperature, and support structures.

4. **Generating G-code:** Translating the model and settings into G-code, which contains the commands for the printer's movements and actions.

Popular Slicing Software:

1. **Cura:** Open-source software known for its user-friendly interface and robust features.

2. **PrusaSlicer:** Developed by Prusa Research, it's highly customizable and supports a wide range of printers.

3. **Simplify3D:** A commercial option that offers advanced features and fine control over print settings.

4. **Slic3r:** Another open-source option with extensive customization capabilities.

3D – Printer Configurations

1. Printer Types:

- **FDM (Fused Deposition Modeling):** Most common and affordable, uses thermoplastic filaments.

- **SLA (Stereolithography):** Uses resin and a UV laser to cure layers, producing high-detail prints.

- **SLS (Selective Laser Sintering):** Uses a laser to fuse powder materials, good for complex geometries.

- **DMLS (Direct Metal Laser Sintering):** Similar to SLS but used for metal powders.

2. Key Printer Settings:

- **Layer Height:** Determines the resolution and surface finish of the print. Smaller layers yield higher quality but take longer to print.

- **Print Speed:** Balances print time and quality. Higher speeds can reduce quality.

- **Infill Density:** The internal structure of the print, affecting strength and material usage. Common values range from 10% to 100%.

- **Nozzle Temperature:** Crucial for proper filament extrusion. Each material has an optimal temperature range.

- **Bed Temperature:** Helps with print adhesion and preventing warping. Important for materials like ABS.

- **Retraction Settings:** Reduces stringing and oozing by retracting filament during non-print moves.

Working with Cura

Cura Overview: Cura, developed by Ultimaker, is a widely-used open-source slicing software that supports many 3D printers. It offers an intuitive interface with powerful features for beginners and advanced users alike.

Steps to Use Cura:

1. **Download and Install Cura:**

   o Download the latest version from the Ultimaker website.

   o Install it by following the on-screen instructions.

2. **Setup and Configuration:**

   o **Add Your Printer:**

     ▪ Open Cura and go to Preferences > Printers > Add Printer.

     ▪ Select your printer model from the list or add a custom printer by entering the necessary details (build volume, nozzle size, etc.).

   o **Configure Print Settings:**

     ▪ Select your printer from the Printer dropdown menu.

     ▪ Click on the Print Setup panel to configure basic settings such as layer height, infill density, and support structures.

3. **Import and Prepare 3D Model:**

   - **Import Model:**

     - Click on Open File and select your 3D model file (STL, OBJ, or 3MF).

   - **Position Model:**

     - Use the Move, Scale, Rotate, and Mirror tools to adjust the model's position on the build plate.

   - **Print Setup:**

     - Adjust settings like layer height, wall thickness, infill density, and support generation in the Print Setup panel.

     - Use the Recommended mode for basic settings or switch to Custom for more advanced options.

4. **Generate G-code:**

   - Click Slice to generate the G-code.

   - Review the estimated print time and material usage.

   - Click Save to File or directly save to an SD card or USB drive.

5. **Print the Model:**

   - Insert the SD card or USB drive into your 3D printer.

   - Start the print from the printer's interface.

Tips:

- **Profiles:** Save custom profiles for different materials and print types.

- **Plug-in:** Explore Cura's marketplace for additional plugins to enhance functionality.

- **Preview:** Use the layer view to preview the sliced model and ensure there are no issues.

Working with PrusaSlicer

PrusaSlicer Overview: PrusaSlicer, developed by Prusa Research, is a powerful, open-source slicing software tailored for Prusa 3D printers but also supports many other models. It offers extensive customization and advanced features.

Steps to Use PrusaSlicer:

1. **Download and Install PrusaSlicer:**

   o Download the latest version from the Prusa website.

   o Install it by following the on-screen instructions.

2. **Setup and Configuration:**

   o **Add Your Printer:**

     ▪ Open PrusaSlicer and follow the Configuration Wizard to select your printer model or add a custom printer.

   o **Configure Print Settings:**

     ▪ Set up the basic parameters for your printer such as build volume and nozzle size.

3. **Import and Prepare 3D Model:**

   o **Import Model:**

     ▪ Click on Add and select your 3D model file (STL, OBJ, or 3MF).

   o **Position Model:**

- Use the Move, Scale, Rotate, and Cut tools to adjust the model's position on the build plate.

  o **Print Settings:**

    - Choose from predefined print settings or create custom ones by adjusting parameters like layer height, perimeters, infill, and supports.

    - PrusaSlicer offers modes such as Simple, Advanced, and Expert to cater to different skill levels.

4. **Generate G-code:**

   o Click Slice Now to generate the G-code.

   o Review the estimated print time and material usage in the right-hand panel.

   o Click Export G-code to save the file.

5. **Print the Model:**

   o Transfer the G-code file to your printer using an SD card or USB drive.

   o Start the print from the printer's interface.

Tips:

- **Profiles:** Utilize the default profiles optimized for Prusa printers or create custom profiles for other printers.

- **Multi-material:** If using a multi-material printer, set up multi-material profiles and assign materials to different parts of the model.

- **Support Structures:** Fine-tune support settings to optimize removal and print quality.

Common Features and Best Practices

1. Layer Height:

- **Fine Detail:** Use a smaller layer height (e.g., 0.1mm) for high-detail prints.

- **Faster Prints:** Use a larger layer height (e.g., 0.2mm) for quicker prints with less detail.

2. Infill Density:

- **Strength:** Higher infill density (e.g., 50-100%) for strong parts.

- **Material Savings:** Lower infill density (e.g., 10-20%) for lightweight parts.

3. Print Speed:

- Balance speed with quality. Faster speeds reduce print time but may lower print quality.

4. Supports:

- **Auto-generate supports** for overhangs and bridges.

- Adjust support density and pattern for ease of removal.

5. Bed Adhesion:

- Use settings like brim or raft to improve bed adhesion for models with small footprints.

6. BUSINESS SECTORS

By understanding following elements and carefully planning your approach, you can set a solid foundation for a successful additive manufacturing business.

How to Start Additive Manufacturing Business

1. Market Research:

- Identify potential markets and industries that could benefit from 3D printing services.

- Analyze competitors and understand their offerings and pricing.

2. Business Plan:

- Define your business model (e.g., on-demand printing, product development, custom parts).

- Outline startup costs, ongoing expenses, and revenue projections.

3. Equipment and Software:

- Invest in reliable 3D printers that suit your target market's needs.

- Choose slicing software that provides the necessary features and ease of use for your team.

- Consider additional software for design (CAD software) and post-processing.

4. Materials:

- Source high-quality filaments, resins, or powders depending on your printer types.

- Maintain an inventory of commonly used materials and experiment with new ones.

5. Training and Skills:

- Ensure you and your team are proficient in 3D modeling, slicing software, and printer maintenance.

- Stay updated with industry trends and advancements.

6. Quality Control:

- Develop a system for checking the quality of prints before delivery.

- Understand the tolerances and limitations of your equipment.

7. Marketing and Sales:

- Create a website showcasing your services and portfolio.

- Utilize social media, online advertising, and networking to attract clients.

- Consider partnerships with local businesses or educational institutions.

8. Legal and Safety Considerations:

- Ensure compliance with local regulations regarding manufacturing and business operations.

- Implement safety measures for handling materials and operating printers.

Additive manufacturing, commonly known as 3D printing, has significantly impacted the market for customizable gifts and home decor. This technology enables the creation of personalized, unique items with intricate designs that are difficult or impossible to achieve with traditional manufacturing methods. Here's how additive manufacturing is revolutionizing this sector:

Customizable Gifts and Home Decors

1. Personalized Items:

- **Jewelry:** Custom rings, bracelets, and necklaces can be designed to include names, initials, or special dates.

- **Keepsakes:** Items like key chains, ornaments, and photo frames can be tailored with personal messages or images.

- **Gadgets and Accessories:** Personalized phone cases, watch straps, and desk accessories are popular choices.

2. Rapid Prototyping and Production:

- **One-off Creations:** 3D printing allows for the efficient production of single or limited edition items without the need for expensive molds or tooling.

- **Quick Turnaround:** Designs can be quickly modified and produced, making it ideal for last-minute gifts.

3. Unique and Custom Designs:

- **Tailor-Made:** Gifts can be designed to suit the recipient's preferences, hobbies, or interests, such as custom figurines, puzzles, or model kits.

- **Collaborative Design:** Customers can be involved in the design process, providing input to create truly personalized gifts.

4. Materials and Finishes:

- **Variety of Materials:** Use of different materials like plastics, metals, ceramics, and even wood composites to create unique textures and finishes.

- **Post-Processing:** Items can be painted, polished, or coated to enhance their appearance and durability.

Home Decor

1. Custom Furniture and Fixtures:

- **Unique Designs:** Custom tables, chairs, and light fixtures can be designed to fit specific spaces or aesthetic preferences.

- **Functional Decor:** Items like custom shelving, planters, and organizers that are both decorative and functional.

2. Art and Sculptures:

- **Bespoke Art Pieces:** Artists can create intricate, personalized sculptures, wall art, and installations that are unique to each client.

- **Reproduction:** 3D printing allows for the replication of famous artworks with modifications or customizations.

3. Personalized Home Accessories:

- **Decorative Items:** Custom vases, bowls, picture frames, and candle holders that match the decor style of a home.

- **Textiles:** 3D printed fabrics and patterns for cushions, curtains, and other soft furnishings.

4. Architectural Elements:

- **Custom Tiles and Panels:** Unique designs for wall tiles, floor tiles, and decorative panels.

- **Hardware:** Custom door handles, knobs, and other fixtures that add a personal touch to interiors.

Advantages of Additive Manufacturing in Customizable Gifts and Home Decor

1. Design Flexibility:

- Complex geometries and intricate designs can be easily created without the limitations of traditional manufacturing.

2. Cost-Effective:

- Economical for producing small batches or one-off items, eliminating the need for costly molds and tooling.

3. Speed:

- Rapid production and prototyping allow for quick iterations and faster time-to-market for new designs.

4. Sustainability:

- Reduced material waste and the ability to use eco-friendly materials contribute to more sustainable production practices.

5. Personalization:

- High level of customization to meet individual customer preferences and requirements.

6. Innovation:

- Continuous advancements in 3D printing technologies and materials expand the possibilities for new and innovative products.

Examples and Use Cases

1. Online Customization Platforms:

- Websites that allow customers to customize and order 3D printed gifts and decor items, such as Shapeways and Etsy shops offering 3D printed products.

2. In-Store Customization:

- Retail stores with 3D printing kiosks where customers can design and print custom items on-site.

3. Bespoke Interior Design:

- Interior designers using 3D printing to create custom decor elements tailored to clients' homes.

4. Small Business and Artisans:

- Independent artists and small businesses leveraging 3D printing to offer unique, personalized products that stand out in the market.

Additive manufacturing enables the creation of highly customizable gifts and home decor, providing a unique blend of personalization, design freedom, and efficiency. This has opened up new opportunities for creativity and innovation in the market, catering to the growing demand for personalized and unique products.

Fashion

Additive manufacturing, commonly known as 3D printing, has made significant strides in the fashion industry, offering new possibilities for designers, manufacturers, and consumers. Here's how additive manufacturing is revolutionizing fashion:

1. Customizable and Unique Designs

1.1 Personalized Fashion:

- **Custom Fit:** 3D scanning technology can capture precise body measurements, allowing for the creation of perfectly fitting clothing and accessories.

- **Personalized Styles:** Consumers can personalize designs, colors, and patterns, resulting in one-of-a-kind fashion pieces.

1.2 Innovative Textures and Patterns:

- **Complex Geometries:** 3D printing allows designers to create intricate patterns and textures that are difficult or impossible to achieve with traditional methods.

- **Unique Materials:** New materials such as flexible filaments, metallic finishes, and composite materials expand the range of textures and finishes available.

2. Sustainable and Ethical Fashion

2.1 Waste Reduction:

- **On-Demand Production:** 3D printing produces items as needed, reducing overproduction and waste associated with mass manufacturing.

- **Material Efficiency:** Additive manufacturing uses only the material necessary for the item, minimizing waste.

2.2 Recycling and Eco-Friendly Materials:

- **Recycled Filaments:** Some 3D printers use filaments made from recycled plastics, contributing to a circular economy.

- **Biodegradable Materials:** Innovations in biodegradable materials offer more sustainable options for fashion production.

3. Prototyping and Rapid Iteration

3.1 Faster Prototyping:

- **Design Iteration:** Designers can quickly prototype and test new designs, allowing for rapid iteration and refinement.

- **Cost-Effective Samples:** Producing samples with 3D printing is more cost-effective compared to traditional methods, facilitating more experimental and creative designs.

3.2 Market Testing:

- **Limited Runs:** Designers can produce limited runs of new designs to test market response before committing to larger production runs.

4. Accessories and Footwear

4.1 Jewelry and Accessories:

- **Custom Jewelry:** 3D printing allows for highly detailed and customized jewelry designs, including rings, necklaces, bracelets, and earrings.

- **Fashion Accessories:** Customizable sunglasses, handbags, belts, and other accessories can be produced with 3D printing.

4.2 Footwear:

- **Custom-Fit Shoes:** 3D scanning and printing technologies enable the production of custom-fit shoes, enhancing comfort and performance.

- **Innovative Designs:** Footwear brands are using 3D printing to create innovative designs with unique structures and materials.

5. Haute Couture and Avant-Garde Fashion

5.1 High Fashion:

- **Runway Pieces:** High-fashion designers are using 3D printing to create avant-garde pieces for runway shows, showcasing the artistic potential of the technology.

- **Collaborative Projects:** Collaborations between fashion designers and tech companies are pushing the boundaries of what is possible in fashion design.

5.2 Wearable Technology:

- **Smart Textiles:** Integration of electronics and sensors into 3D printed textiles for creating interactive and functional garments.

- **Performance Wear:** Custom sportswear with embedded sensors to monitor performance and health metrics.

Examples and Use Cases

1. Iris van Herpen:

- Known for her groundbreaking use of 3D printing in haute couture, creating intricate and avant-garde designs that push the boundaries of fashion.

2. Adidas Futurecraft:

- Adidas uses 3D printing for its Futurecraft line, producing custom midsoles tailored to an individual's foot shape and stride.

3. Ministry of Supply:

- This fashion brand uses 3D printing to create seamless, customized knitwear, reducing waste and enhancing fit and comfort.

4. Shapeways and Nervous System:

- Platforms like Shapeways offer customizable 3D printed jewelry and fashion accessories, while Nervous System creates unique, generative design pieces using 3D printing.

5. Heron Preston and Zellerfeld:

- Collaborations like Heron Preston's with Zellerfeld explore 3D printed footwear, pushing the envelope in sustainable and customizable shoe design.

Challenges and Future Prospects

Challenges:

- **Material Limitations:** The range of materials suitable for 3D printing in fashion is still growing, with ongoing research needed to expand options.

- **Production Speed:** 3D printing can be slower compared to traditional manufacturing, making it less suitable for mass production.

- **Durability and Comfort:** Ensuring that 3D printed garments and accessories meet durability and comfort standards is crucial.

Future Prospects:

- **Material Innovation:** Development of new materials, including smart and sustainable options, will broaden the applications of 3D printing in fashion.

- **Technological Advancements:** Improvements in 3D printing technology will enhance production speed, quality, and cost-effectiveness.

- **Mainstream Adoption:** As costs decrease and technology improves, 3D printing is likely to become more prevalent in mainstream fashion, offering more customized and sustainable options to consumers.

Additive manufacturing is transforming the fashion industry by enabling customization, reducing waste, and fostering innovation in design and materials. As technology continues to advance, its impact on fashion will likely grow, offering exciting possibilities for designers and consumers alike.

Healthcare

Additive manufacturing, commonly known as 3D printing, has become a transformative technology in the healthcare industry. It offers numerous applications ranging from custom prosthetics and implants to advanced surgical models and bio printing. Here's a detailed look at how additive manufacturing is involved in healthcare:

1. Custom Prosthetics and Orthotics

1.1 Personalized Prosthetics:

- **Custom Fit:** 3D scanning and printing allow for the creation of prosthetics tailored to the exact anatomy of the patient, ensuring a perfect fit and increased comfort.

- **Rapid Production:** Prosthetics can be produced quickly and cost-effectively, making them more accessible, especially in low-resource settings.

1.2 Orthotic Devices:

- **Custom Braces:** Orthotic braces for conditions such as scoliosis can be customized to the patient's body shape, providing better support and comfort.

- **Foot Orthotics:** Custom insoles and orthopedic footwear can be produced to address specific foot conditions.

2. Implants and Surgical Instruments

2.1 Customized Implants:

- **Bone Implants:** 3D printing enables the production of patient-specific implants for bones, such as cranial plates, hip joints, and spinal implants, that match the patient's anatomy.

- **Dental Implants:** Customized dental implants and crowns can be precisely manufactured to fit individual patients.

2.2 Surgical Instruments:

- **Custom Tools:** Surgeons can design and produce custom surgical instruments tailored to specific procedures, improving precision and outcomes.

- **Single-Use Instruments:** 3D printing allows for the cost-effective production of single-use instruments, reducing the risk of infection.

3. Surgical Planning and Education

3.1 Surgical Models:

- **Pre-Surgical Planning:** 3D printed models of patient-specific anatomy based on CT or MRI scans help surgeons plan complex procedures more effectively.

- **Simulation:** Surgeons can practice on realistic models, improving their skills and reducing the risk during actual surgery.

3.2 Educational Tools:

- **Anatomical Models:** Medical students and professionals can use 3D printed models to study and understand complex anatomy and surgical techniques.

- **Patient Communication:** 3D models help doctors explain medical conditions and surgical procedures to patients, improving understanding and consent.

4. Bio printing and Tissue Engineering

4.1 Bio printing:

- **Tissue Engineering:** Researchers are developing bioprinting techniques to create tissues and organs using living cells. This could eventually lead to lab-grown organs for transplants.

- **Drug Testing:** 3D printed tissue models can be used for drug testing and research, reducing the need for animal testing and improving the relevance of results to human biology.

4.2 Regenerative Medicine:

- **Scaffolds for Tissue Growth:** 3D printing can produce scaffolds that support the growth of new tissues, aiding in the repair of damaged organs and tissues.

5. Pharmaceutical Applications

5.1 Custom Medications:

- **Personalized Dosage Forms:** 3D printing allows for the production of medications with personalized dosages and release profiles, tailored to the specific needs of individual patients.

- **Polypills:** Multiple drugs can be combined into a single pill, simplifying medication regimens for patients with multiple prescriptions.

5.2 Rapid Prototyping:

- **Drug Development:** 3D printing accelerates the development and testing of new drug formulations, reducing time-to-market for new medications.

Advantages of Additive Manufacturing in Healthcare

1. Personalization:

- High degree of customization to fit individual patient needs, improving the effectiveness and comfort of medical devices and treatments.

2. Speed:

- Faster production times compared to traditional manufacturing methods, allowing for rapid prototyping and production.

3. Cost-Effectiveness:

- Reduced costs for producing custom and complex medical devices, making advanced healthcare solutions more accessible.

4. Innovation:

- Facilitates the development of new medical devices, treatments, and techniques, driving innovation in the healthcare industry.

Challenges and Future Prospects

Challenges:

- **Regulatory Approval:** Ensuring that 3D printed medical devices meet stringent regulatory standards for safety and efficacy.

- **Material Limitations:** Ongoing research is needed to develop new materials suitable for medical applications, including biocompatible and bioresorbable materials.

- **Technical Expertise:** Requires specialized knowledge and skills to design and produce effective 3D printed medical devices.

Future Prospects:

- **Advanced Bio printing:** Continued advancements in bio printing could lead to the production of functional tissues and organs, addressing the shortage of donor organs.

- **Integration with Digital Health:** Combining 3D printing with digital health technologies, such as AI and IoT, to create smart, connected medical devices.

- **Widespread Adoption:** As technology matures and becomes more cost-effective, 3D printing is likely to see broader adoption in mainstream healthcare.

Additive manufacturing is revolutionizing healthcare by enabling personalized, efficient, and innovative solutions. Its applications span across prosthetics, implants, surgical planning, bio printing, and pharmaceuticals, offering significant benefits to patients and healthcare providers alike. As technology continues to evolve, its impact on healthcare will only grow, paving the way for new treatments and improved patient outcomes.

Automotive

Additive manufacturing, commonly known as 3D printing, has significantly influenced the automotive industry by providing new ways to design, produce, and customize vehicle components. Here's a detailed look at how additive manufacturing is involved in the automotive sector:

1. Prototyping and Product Development

1.1 Rapid Prototyping:

- **Accelerated Design Iteration:** 3D printing allows for quick production of prototypes, enabling faster design iterations and testing.
- **Cost Efficiency:** Reduces the costs associated with traditional prototyping methods, such as tooling and molds.

1.2 Functional Prototypes:

- **Testing and Validation:** Functional prototypes can be produced to test the fit, form, and function of parts in real-world conditions.
- **Complex Geometry:** Enables the creation of complex geometries that are difficult or impossible to achieve with traditional manufacturing.

2. Customization and Personalization

2.1 Custom Parts:

- **Interior Customization:** Personalized interior components, such as dashboard panels, gear knobs, and custom trims.
- **Exterior Customization:** Custom grilles, badges, and body parts tailored to specific customer preferences.

2.2 Aftermarket and Spare Parts:

- **On-Demand Production:** Allows for the on-demand production of spare parts, reducing inventory costs and lead times.
- **Obsolete Parts:** Enables the production of parts for older or discontinued models that are no longer available through traditional supply chains.

3. Tooling and Manufacturing Aids

3.1 Custom Tools and Fixtures:

- **Specialized Tools:** Custom jigs, fixtures, and assembly tools can be produced to improve manufacturing efficiency and accuracy.
- **Rapid Tooling:** Allows for the quick production of tooling components, reducing lead times in the manufacturing process.

3.2 Production Aids:

- **Ergonomics:** Custom ergonomic tools and aids can be designed to improve worker comfort and safety.
- **Quality Control:** Custom gauges and measurement tools for quality control processes.

4. Lightweight and Complex Components

4.1 Lightweight Structures:

- **Material Optimization:** 3D printing allows for the creation of lightweight structures with optimized material use, reducing vehicle weight and improving fuel efficiency.
- **Topology Optimization:** Advanced design techniques can be used to create parts with optimal strength-to-weight ratios.

4.2 Complex Assemblies:

- **Integrated Functions:** Parts with integrated functions, such as built-in channels for wiring or fluid passage, reducing the need for multiple components.
- **Reduced Assembly Time:** Complex assemblies can be printed as single parts, reducing assembly time and complexity.

5. End-Use Parts

5.1 Production Parts:

- **Direct Manufacturing:** Some parts, especially low-volume or highly specialized components, can be directly manufactured using 3D printing.
- **Batch Production:** Suitable for producing small batches of parts, such as limited edition or niche market vehicles.

5.2 High-Performance Parts:

- **Performance Enhancements:** Parts designed for high performance, such as custom exhaust systems, air intake manifolds, and turbochargers.
- **Motorsports:** Widely used in motorsports for producing bespoke components that meet specific performance criteria.

6. Sustainability

6.1 Material Efficiency:

- **Reduced Waste:** Additive manufacturing uses only the material needed for the part, significantly reducing material waste compared to subtractive methods.
- **Recyclable Materials:** Development of recyclable and bio-based materials for more sustainable production.

6.2 Energy Efficiency:

- **Efficient Manufacturing:** Additive manufacturing processes can be more energy-efficient, especially for low-volume production.

Examples and Use Cases

1. Ford:

- Ford uses 3D printing for prototyping and producing certain end-use parts, such as intake manifolds and lightweight brackets.

2. BMW:

- BMW has integrated 3D printing into its production line for creating tools, fixtures, and end-use parts, particularly in its i8 Roadster and MINI models.

3. Volkswagen:

- Volkswagen uses additive manufacturing for producing prototypes, tooling, and custom components for various models.

4. General Motors:

- GM employs 3D printing for rapid prototyping, production aids, and developing innovative parts like the lightweight seat brackets in the Cadillac CT4-V Blackwing.

5. Bugatti:

- Bugatti utilizes 3D printing for producing high-performance parts, such as titanium brake calipers and complex structures in their hypercars.

Challenges and Future Prospects

Challenges:

- **Material Limitations:** The range of materials suitable for automotive applications is expanding but still limited compared to traditional manufacturing.

- **Production Speed:** Additive manufacturing can be slower than conventional methods, making it less suitable for high-volume production.
- **Regulatory Compliance:** Ensuring that 3D printed parts meet industry standards and regulatory requirements is crucial.

Future Prospects:
- **Material Innovation:** Continued development of new materials, including high-performance polymers and metals, will broaden the applications in the automotive industry.
- **Integration with Traditional Manufacturing:** Hybrid approaches combining additive and subtractive manufacturing techniques will enhance production capabilities.
- **Mass Customization:** As technology advances, 3D printing will enable more widespread adoption of mass customization in automotive manufacturing.
- **Sustainability Initiatives:** Additive manufacturing will play a key role in creating more sustainable production processes and developing eco-friendly vehicles.

Additive manufacturing is revolutionizing the automotive industry by enabling rapid prototyping, customization, light weighting, and the production of complex and high-performance components. As the technology continues to evolve, its impact on automotive design, manufacturing, and sustainability will only increase, offering exciting opportunities for innovation and efficiency.

Architecture:

Additive manufacturing (AM), commonly known as 3D printing, is increasingly revolutionizing the field of architecture by offering new possibilities for design, construction, and sustainability. This technology enables architects to create complex geometries, reduce construction time, and explore innovative materials. Here's how additive manufacturing is involved in architecture:

1. Design Freedom and Complex Geometries

1.1 Organic Shapes:

- **Freedom of Design:** AM allows architects to design complex, organic shapes and structures that are difficult or impossible to achieve with traditional construction methods.

- **Parametric Design:** Architects can use parametric design tools to optimize designs and create intricate patterns and forms.

1.2 Customization:

- **Tailored Solutions:** Buildings and components can be customized to meet specific site conditions, client preferences, and functional requirements.

- **Personalization:** Individualized designs can be easily adapted and fabricated, offering unique architectural solutions.

2. Rapid Prototyping and Iterative Design

2.1 Scale Models:

- **Quick Iteration:** Architects can rapidly prototype scale models and iterations of their designs, allowing for faster design validation and client feedback.

- **Visualization:** 3D printed models provide a tangible representation of architectural concepts, aiding in communication with clients and stakeholders.

2.2 Iterative Design Process:

- **Design Optimization:** Architects can quickly test and refine designs, exploring multiple iterations to achieve optimal outcomes in terms of aesthetics, performance, and functionality.

3. Construction and Building Components

3.1 Prefabrication:

- **Custom Components:** AM enables the fabrication of prefabricated building components, such as panels, façades, and structural elements, with high precision and minimal waste.

- **On-Site Assembly:** Prefabricated parts can be assembled on-site, reducing construction time and labor costs.

3.2 Complex Structures:

- **Load-Bearing Structures:** 3D printing can create load-bearing walls and columns with intricate internal geometries optimized for strength and material efficiency.

- **Facade Elements:** Decorative and functional façade elements can be produced with detailed textures and patterns, enhancing architectural aesthetics.

4. Sustainable Construction Practices

4.1 Material Efficiency:

- **Reduced Waste:** AM minimizes material waste by using only the necessary amount of material for construction, compared to subtractive manufacturing methods.

- **Recycled Materials:** Recyclable and sustainable materials can be used in AM processes, contributing to environmentally friendly construction practices.

4.2 Energy Efficiency:

- **Insulation Properties:** 3D printed structures can incorporate built-in insulation and energy-efficient features, reducing energy consumption over the building's lifecycle.

- **Passive Design:** Design strategies, such as solar shading and natural ventilation, can be integrated into 3D printed structures to optimize energy performance.

5. Examples and Applications

5.1 Experimental Architecture:

- Architects and designers are using AM to push the boundaries of architectural design, creating avant-garde structures and installations that showcase the potential of additive manufacturing.

5.2 Sustainable Housing:

- Initiatives are underway to use AM for producing affordable and sustainable housing solutions, addressing housing shortages and urbanization challenges.

5.3 Restoration and Preservation:

- Historic buildings and cultural heritage sites can benefit from AM by facilitating the restoration of intricate details and creating accurate replicas of damaged or missing components.

6. Industry Innovations

6.1 MX3D Bridge, Amsterdam:

- MX3D collaborated with designers and engineers to 3D print a stainless steel pedestrian bridge in Amsterdam, demonstrating the feasibility of AM for large-scale architectural projects.

6.2 ICON and 3D Printed Homes:

- ICON, in partnership with housing organizations, is using AM to construct affordable and resilient homes, showcasing the potential of AM in addressing global housing challenges.

Challenges and Future Prospects

Challenges:

- **Scale and Size Limitations:** Current AM technologies have limitations in terms of scale and size, which may restrict their application in larger architectural projects.

- **Regulatory Approval:** Ensuring compliance with building codes and regulations for 3D printed structures remains a challenge in many regions.

- **Material Selection:** Developing suitable construction materials that meet structural and durability requirements for AM applications in architecture.

Future Prospects:

- **Advancements in Technology:** Continued advancements in AM technologies, including larger-scale printers and multi-material capabilities, will expand the scope of architectural applications.

- **Integration with Robotics:** Integration of AM with robotics and automation will further streamline construction processes, enhancing efficiency and precision.

- **Collaborative Design Platforms:** Development of collaborative design platforms and digital fabrication workflows will support architects in leveraging AM for innovative and sustainable architectural solutions.

Additive manufacturing is reshaping architecture by offering architects unprecedented design freedom, efficiency in construction, and sustainable building solutions. As technology continues to evolve, the potential for AM to transform architectural practice and urban design will only grow, ushering in a new era of creativity and sustainability in the built environment.

Aerospace:

Additive manufacturing (AM), commonly known as 3D printing has revolutionized the aerospace industry by enabling the production of complex, lightweight, and high-performance components. This technology offers numerous advantages, including material efficiency, cost savings, and design flexibility. Here's a detailed look at how additive manufacturing is involved in aerospace:

1. Lightweight Structures

1.1 Material Reduction:

- **Optimized Designs:** AM allows for the creation of optimized structures that use less material without compromising strength, reducing the overall weight of aircraft and spacecraft.

- **Honeycomb Structures:** Common in aerospace, these structures provide high strength-to-weight ratios and can be easily produced using 3D printing.

1.2 Fuel Efficiency:

- **Reduced Weight:** Lighter aircraft consume less fuel, which leads to cost savings and lower emissions, enhancing overall efficiency and sustainability.

2. Complex and Customized Parts

2.1 Geometric Complexity:

- **Freedom of Design:** AM enables the production of parts with complex geometries that would be impossible or too costly to manufacture with traditional methods.

- **Integrated Components:** Multiple parts can be combined into a single complex component, reducing the need for assembly and the potential for part failure.

2.2 Customization:

- **Tailored Solutions:** Components can be customized for specific applications, improving performance and fitting exact requirements.

- **Prototyping:** Rapid prototyping allows for quick iteration and testing of custom designs.

3. Reduced Lead Times and Costs

3.1 Rapid Prototyping:

- **Accelerated Development:** AM significantly speeds up the prototyping phase, allowing for faster design validation and iteration.

- **Cost Efficiency:** Reduces the costs associated with traditional tooling and machining, especially for low-volume or highly specialized parts.

3.2 On-Demand Production:

- **Inventory Reduction:** Parts can be produced on demand, reducing the need for large inventories and storage costs.

- **Spare Parts:** Manufacturing spare parts as needed, particularly for legacy systems, helps maintain older aircraft without excessive costs.

4. Improved Performance and Safety

4.1 High-Performance Materials:

- **Advanced Materials:** AM supports the use of high-performance materials such as titanium alloys, nickel-based superalloys, and advanced composites, which offer excellent strength, heat resistance, and durability.

- **Material Gradients:** Functionally graded materials can be produced, where different materials are combined within a single part to enhance performance.

4.2 Enhanced Safety:

- **Consistent Quality:** AM processes, when properly controlled, can produce highly consistent and reliable parts, improving overall safety.

- **Reduced Failures:** Integrated designs and fewer assembly points reduce the risk of mechanical failures.

5. Applications in Aerospace

5.1 Engine Components:

- **Fuel Nozzles:** GE Aviation uses AM to produce fuel nozzles for jet engines, combining multiple parts into a single, more efficient component.

- **Turbine Blades:** Advanced cooling channels can be integrated into turbine blades, improving efficiency and performance.

5.2 Structural Components:

- **Brackets and Fittings:** Lightweight brackets and fittings are commonly produced using AM, reducing weight and maintaining strength.

- **Wing Structures:** Complex wing structures and components can be optimized for weight and strength using 3D printing.

5.3 Interior Components:

- **Cabin Parts:** Customizable and lightweight interior components, such as seat frames and panels, are produced to enhance passenger comfort and reduce weight.

- **Ducting and Ventilation:** Complex ducting and ventilation systems can be efficiently manufactured with AM.

5.4 Space Applications:

- **Satellite Parts:** AM is used to produce components for satellites, where weight reduction is critical.

- **Rocket Engines:** Companies like SpaceX and Rocket Lab use AM for manufacturing rocket engine components, reducing costs and improving performance.

6. Industry Examples

1. GE Aviation:

- GE Aviation has successfully used AM to produce jet engine components, such as fuel nozzles, which are lighter, stronger, and more efficient than traditionally manufactured parts.

2. Boeing:

- Boeing employs AM for producing various aircraft components, including structural and interior parts, to reduce weight and improve performance.

3. Airbus:

- Airbus uses AM for producing lightweight brackets and other structural components in its aircraft, leading to significant weight savings and fuel efficiency improvements.

4. NASA:

- NASA leverages AM for developing components for space exploration, including rocket engine parts and tools for use on the International Space Station.

5. SpaceX:

- SpaceX uses AM to manufacture rocket engine components, such as the SuperDraco engine, enhancing performance and reducing manufacturing time.

Challenges and Future Prospects

Challenges:

- **Material Limitations:** The range of materials suitable for AM in aerospace is expanding but still limited compared to traditional manufacturing.

- **Certification and Standards:** Ensuring that AM parts meet stringent aerospace standards and certifications can be challenging.

- **Process Control:** Maintaining consistent quality and performance in AM processes requires precise control and expertise.

Future Prospects:

- **Material Innovation:** Continued development of new materials, including high-performance metals and composites, will expand the applications of AM in aerospace.

- **Hybrid Manufacturing:** Combining additive and traditional manufacturing techniques will optimize production and enhance capabilities.

- **In-Situ Manufacturing:** On-demand manufacturing of parts in space or at remote locations will become feasible, supporting long-term space missions and reducing dependency on Earth-based supply chains.

- **Sustainability:** AM will play a key role in developing more sustainable aerospace manufacturing processes, reducing waste, and improving fuel efficiency.

Additive manufacturing is transforming the aerospace industry by enabling the production of lightweight, complex, and high-performance components. Its applications span from prototyping to end-use parts, offering significant advantages in design flexibility, cost savings, and sustainability. As technology advances, the impact of AM on aerospace will continue to grow, driving innovation and efficiency in the industry.

Education:

Additive manufacturing, or 3D printing, is increasingly being integrated into education across various levels and disciplines. It offers unique opportunities for enhancing learning, fostering creativity, and preparing students for future careers. Here's a detailed look at how additive manufacturing is involved in education:

1. Enhancing STEM Education

1.1 Hands-On Learning:

- **Practical Applications:** Students can directly engage with STEM concepts by designing and creating physical models, helping them understand abstract concepts more concretely.

- **Problem-Solving Skills:** 3D printing projects encourage critical thinking and problem-solving, as students must design, troubleshoot, and iterate their creations.

1.2 Integrative Learning:

- **Cross-Disciplinary Projects:** Combining elements of science, technology, engineering, and mathematics into cohesive projects, fostering a multidisciplinary approach to learning.

- **Real-World Applications:** Students can see the practical applications of their studies, such as creating prototypes for engineering projects or models for scientific research.

2. Art and Design Education

2.1 Creative Expression:

- **Art Projects:** Students can explore new forms of artistic expression by creating intricate sculptures, jewelry, and other art pieces using 3D printing.

- **Design Prototyping:** Allows for rapid prototyping and iteration in design courses, enabling students to bring their digital designs to life quickly and efficiently.

2.2 Fashion and Textile Design:

- **Custom Fabrics and Accessories:** 3D printing can be used to create custom textiles, accessories, and even clothing, providing fashion students with new tools for innovation.

- **Experimental Materials:** Encourages experimentation with new materials and design techniques.

3. Special Education

3.1 Customized Learning Aids:

- **Tactile Learning Tools:** 3D printed models and aids can help students with disabilities understand complex concepts through touch and manipulation.

- **Adaptive Devices:** Customizable tools and devices can be designed to meet the specific needs of individual students, enhancing their learning experience.

3.2 Inclusive Education:

- **Accessible Materials:** 3D printing can create accessible educational materials, such as braille books and tactile maps, promoting inclusive education.

4. Higher Education and Research

4.1 Engineering and Architecture:

- **Prototyping and Testing:** Engineering and architecture students can use 3D printing to create and test prototypes, improving their design and engineering skills.

- **Complex Models:** Enables the creation of complex models and structures that would be difficult to construct with traditional methods.

4.2 Scientific Research:

- **Custom Lab Equipment:** Researchers can design and print custom lab equipment and components, reducing costs and lead times.

- **Bio printing:** Advancements in bio printing allow for the creation of tissue models for medical research and experimentation.

5. Vocational and Technical Training

5.1 Skill Development:

- **Industry-Relevant Skills:** Provides students with hands-on experience in using 3D printing technology, preparing them for careers in various industries, including manufacturing, automotive, aerospace, and healthcare.

- **CNC and CAD Training:** Students learn computer-aided design (CAD) and computer numerical control (CNC) skills, which are highly relevant in the modern workforce.

5.2 Rapid Prototyping:

- **Design to Production:** Students can go through the entire process of designing, prototyping, and producing a part, mirroring real-world manufacturing workflows.

6. Curriculum Development and Innovation

6.1 Interactive Curriculum:

- **Engaging Lessons:** 3D printing can make lessons more engaging and interactive, helping to maintain student interest and enthusiasm.

- **Project-Based Learning:** Encourages project-based learning, where students apply their knowledge to real-world problems and projects.

6.2 Teacher Training:

- **Professional Development:** Provides teachers with training in 3D printing technology, enabling them to integrate it effectively into their classrooms.

- **Curriculum Resources:** Development of curriculum resources and lesson plans that incorporate 3D printing into various subjects.

Examples and Use Cases

1. MakerBot in Schools:

- MakerBot provides 3D printers and curriculum resources to schools, helping to integrate 3D printing into classrooms and enhance STEM education.

2. Tinkercad and Thingiverse:

- These platforms offer easy-to-use tools and a vast library of 3D printable designs, enabling students and teachers to create and share their projects.

3. University Labs:

- Many universities have dedicated 3D printing labs where students and researchers can access advanced 3D printing equipment and materials for their projects.

4. Special Education Programs:

- Programs that use 3D printing to create customized educational aids and adaptive devices for students with special needs.

Challenges and Future Prospects

Challenges:

- **Cost and Accessibility:** While the cost of 3D printers has decreased, there are still budget constraints for many educational institutions.

- **Technical Expertise:** Requires investment in training for teachers and students to effectively use and maintain 3D printing equipment.

- **Integration into Curriculum:** Developing and integrating 3D printing projects into existing curricula can be challenging.

Future Prospects:

- **Broader Accessibility:** As costs continue to decrease, 3D printing technology will become more accessible to a wider range of schools and educational institutions.

- **Advanced Materials:** Development of new, safer, and more sustainable materials for educational use.

- **Curriculum Integration:** Continued development of curriculum resources and training programs to help educators integrate 3D printing into their teaching.

Additive manufacturing is transforming education by providing new ways to enhance learning, foster creativity, and prepare students for future careers. Its applications in STEM, art and design, special education, higher education, vocational training, and curriculum development offer exciting possibilities for innovation and engagement in the classroom. As technology continues to evolve, its impact on education will only grow, creating more opportunities for students and educators alike.

Use cases and Examples

Certainly! Additive manufacturing (AM), commonly known as 3D printing is making significant strides across various sectors in India, driven by innovation, cost-effectiveness, and customization capabilities. Here are some notable examples and use cases of additive manufacturing categorized by sectors in India:

1. Healthcare Sector

1.1 Prosthetics and Orthotics:

- **Customized Prosthetics:** Companies like 3D Usher and Ayu Devices use 3D printing to create affordable and customized prosthetic limbs tailored to individual patients.

- **Orthotic Devices:** Orthopedic braces and supports can be 3D printed to fit patients' anatomical requirements precisely.

1.2 Medical Models and Surgical Planning:

- **Patient-specific Models:** Hospitals and medical institutions use 3D printing to create accurate anatomical models for surgical planning, education, and training.

- **Implant Manufacturing:** Companies like Anatomiz3D and 3D LifePrints India produce patient-specific implants and surgical guides using AM technology.

2. Aerospace and Defense Sector

2.1 UAVs and Drones:

- **Customized Components:** Indian startups and research institutions use 3D printing for manufacturing lightweight components for UAVs (Unmanned Aerial Vehicles) and drones.

- **Aerospace Prototyping:** Organizations like HAL (Hindustan Aeronautics Limited) utilize AM for rapid prototyping of aerospace parts and components.

2.2 Satellite Components:

- **ISRO (Indian Space Research Organisation):** ISRO integrates additive manufacturing for producing satellite components, such as brackets, mounts, and antenna supports, for space missions.

3. Automotive Sector

3.1 Customized Automotive Parts:

- **Rapid Prototyping:** Automotive companies like Tata Motors and Mahindra & Mahindra utilize 3D printing for rapid prototyping of vehicle parts, reducing lead times and costs.

- **End-use Components:** Select components, such as tooling fixtures and interior elements, are increasingly being 3D printed to enhance vehicle performance and customization.

4. Education and Research Sector

4.1 Academic Institutions:

- **IITs and Research Labs:** Indian Institutes of Technology (IITs) and other research institutions use 3D printing for academic research, student projects, and developing prototypes across various disciplines.

- **STEM Education:** Schools and educational institutions integrate 3D printing into STEM (Science, Technology, Engineering, and Mathematics) education to promote hands-on learning and innovation.

5. Architecture and Construction Sector

5.1 Prototyping and Model Making:

- **Architectural Firms:** Design studios and architectural firms in India use 3D printing for creating scale models, intricate architectural elements, and prototypes of building components.

- **Customized Housing Solutions:** Startups like Tvasta Manufacturing Solutions focus on using AM for sustainable and affordable housing solutions, addressing housing challenges in urban and rural areas.

6. Consumer Goods and Art Sector

6.1 Jewelry and Fashion:

- **Custom Jewelry:** Indian artisans and designers leverage 3D printing for creating intricate and customizable jewelry pieces, blending traditional craftsmanship with modern technology.

- **Artistic Creations:** Artists and sculptors explore 3D printing for producing unique artworks and sculptures, showcasing the intersection of art and technology.

7. Industrial Manufacturing Sector

7.1 Tooling and Prototyping:

- **Manufacturing Enterprises:** Industrial firms utilize 3D printing for producing tooling, jigs, and fixtures that enhance production efficiency and precision.

- **Customized Components:** AM enables the production of specialized industrial components with complex geometries and material properties optimized for specific applications.

8. Environmental and Sustainable Development Sector

8.1 Waste Management Solutions:

- **Recycling Initiatives:** Companies explore AM for creating recycled materials and products, contributing to sustainable development goals and environmental conservation efforts.

- **Water Filtration:** 3D printing is used to create innovative water filtration systems and devices that address local water quality issues and improve access to clean water.

9. Arts and Culture Sector

9.1 Museum and Heritage Conservation:

- **Replication and Restoration:** 3D scanning and printing technologies are employed for replicating cultural artifacts and restoring heritage structures, preserving India's rich cultural heritage.

- **Creative Installations:** Artists and designers use 3D printing to create interactive installations and immersive experiences that engage audiences and promote cultural innovation.

10. Government and Public Sector Initiatives

10.1 Smart Cities and Urban Planning:

- **Infrastructure Development:** Additive manufacturing technologies are explored for creating smart city solutions, including customized urban furniture, sustainable housing, and infrastructure components.

- **Public Services:** Governments leverage AM for producing customized tools and equipment for public services, disaster response, and healthcare facilities, enhancing operational efficiency and service delivery.

These examples illustrate how additive manufacturing is transforming industries in India, driving innovation, sustainability, and economic growth. As technology continues to advance, the adoption of 3D printing is expected to expand further, unlocking new possibilities and applications across diverse sectors.

7. ARTIFICIAL INTELLIGENCE IN ADDITIVE MANUFACTURING

AI, or Artificial Intelligence, refers to the simulation of human intelligence in machines that are programmed to think and learn like humans. It encompasses a broad range of technologies and applications that enable machines to perform tasks that typically require human intelligence, such as visual perception, speech recognition, decision-making, and problem-solving.

Key Characteristics of AI:

1. **Machine Learning:** AI systems often employ machine learning algorithms to analyze data, learn from patterns, and make decisions or predictions without explicit programming.

2. **Natural Language Processing (NLP):** NLP enables machines to understand, interpret, and generate human language, facilitating communication between humans and computers.

3. **Computer Vision:** AI systems equipped with computer vision can perceive and interpret visual information from the world, enabling tasks like image recognition, object detection, and facial recognition.

4. **Robotics:** AI-driven robotics combines sensors, actuators, and intelligent algorithms to automate tasks and interact physically with the environment.

Types of AI:

- **Narrow AI (Weak AI):** AI designed to perform specific tasks or solve particular problems, such as voice assistants (e.g., Siri, Alexa), recommendation systems, and autonomous vehicles.

- **General AI (Strong AI):** Hypothetical AI that exhibits human-like intelligence across a wide range of tasks, potentially surpassing human capabilities in cognitive functions.

Applications of AI:

- **Healthcare:** AI aids in medical diagnosis, personalized treatment planning, drug discovery, and patient monitoring.

- **Finance:** AI algorithms analyze financial data for fraud detection, investment strategies, and risk assessment.

- **Retail:** AI powers recommendation engines, customer service chatbots, inventory management, and supply chain optimization.

- **Manufacturing:** AI enhances automation, predictive maintenance, quality control, and adaptive robotics in manufacturing processes.

- **Education:** AI supports personalized learning experiences, adaptive tutoring systems, and educational analytics.

Challenges and Considerations:

- **Ethics and Bias:** Ensuring AI systems are fair, unbiased, and aligned with ethical principles.

- **Privacy and Security:** Safeguarding personal data and preventing AI-driven cyber threats.

- **Jobs and Workforce:** Addressing the impact of automation on jobs and the need for upskilling in AI-related fields.

AI continues to evolve rapidly, shaping various aspects of society and driving innovation across industries. As advancements continue, understanding AI's capabilities, limitations, and ethical implications remains crucial for its responsible deployment and integration into everyday life.

Why AI in AM?

AI (Artificial Intelligence) is increasingly integrated into additive manufacturing (AM), also known as 3D printing, to enhance efficiency, quality, and innovation across various stages of the manufacturing process. Here are several ways AI is leveraged in additive manufacturing:

1. Design Optimization

AI algorithms can analyze vast amounts of data and generate optimized designs for additive manufacturing. This includes:

- **Generative Design:** AI algorithms can create design alternatives based on specified parameters and performance criteria, optimizing for weight, strength, and material usage.

- **Topology Optimization:** AI helps in generating complex and lightweight structures that are well-suited for additive manufacturing processes, minimizing material usage while maintaining structural integrity.

2. Process Monitoring and Control

AI is used to monitor and control additive manufacturing processes in real-time, ensuring quality and consistency:

- **Quality Assurance:** AI algorithms analyze sensor data (e.g., temperature, pressure) during printing to detect anomalies and defects, enabling early intervention and improving yield rates.

- **Predictive Maintenance:** AI predicts equipment maintenance needs based on usage patterns and sensor data, minimizing downtime and optimizing production schedules.

3. Material Development and Selection

AI assists in material research and development for additive manufacturing:

- **Material Modeling:** AI algorithms simulate material behavior under different printing conditions, aiding in the development of new materials with desired properties (e.g., strength, flexibility).

- **Material Selection:** AI helps in choosing the optimal material for specific applications and requirements, considering factors such as cost, performance, and environmental impact.

4. Workflow Automation

AI streamlines additive manufacturing workflows and enhances operational efficiency:

- **Scheduling and Optimization:** AI algorithms optimize production schedules, batch sizes, and resource allocation to maximize throughput and minimize costs.

- **Supply Chain Management:** AI-enabled systems manage inventory levels, procurement, and logistics, ensuring timely availability of materials and components.

5. Post-Processing and Finishing

AI improves post-processing and finishing processes after additive manufacturing:

- **Surface Quality Enhancement:** AI algorithms analyze surface defects and imperfections, guiding automated polishing and finishing processes to achieve desired surface finishes.

- **Assembly and Integration:** AI assists in automated assembly tasks by analyzing part geometries and tolerances, ensuring accurate fit and alignment of components.

6. Customization and Personalization

AI enables mass customization and personalized manufacturing through additive manufacturing:

- **Design Customization:** AI-driven tools create customized designs and adaptations for individualized products, such as medical implants and consumer goods.

- **Real-time Adaptation:** AI adjusts manufacturing parameters in real-time based on customer preferences or design modifications, facilitating on-demand production.

7. Sustainability and Waste Reduction

AI supports sustainable practices in additive manufacturing:

- **Material Efficiency:** AI optimizes material usage and minimizes waste by generating minimalistic designs and intelligent support structures.

- **Energy Optimization:** AI algorithms optimize energy consumption during printing processes, reducing environmental impact and operational costs.

Future Directions

As AI and additive manufacturing technologies continue to advance, their integration is expected to lead to further innovations, such as:

- **AI-driven AM Platforms:** Integrated platforms that combine AI with additive manufacturing technologies to offer end-to-end solutions from design to production.

- **Autonomous Manufacturing:** AI-powered autonomous systems that can self-optimize and self-correct during the additive manufacturing process without human intervention.

The synergy between AI and additive manufacturing holds promise for transforming manufacturing industries, offering enhanced capabilities in design flexibility, production efficiency, and product customization while driving advancements in sustainability and quality assurance.

AI – Products

AI-based 3D printed products showcase the integration of artificial intelligence with additive manufacturing technologies, leading to innovative solutions across various industries. Here are some notable examples:

1. Customized Prosthetics and Orthotics

Example: UNYQ

- **Application:** UNYQ utilizes AI-driven design tools to create personalized prosthetic covers and orthotic devices tailored to individual patient needs.

- **Technology:** AI algorithms generate customized designs based on patient measurements and preferences, optimizing fit, comfort, and aesthetics.

2. Generatively Designed Aerospace Components

Example: Airbus

- **Application:** Airbus leverages generative design powered by AI to develop lightweight and optimized aerospace components using additive manufacturing.

- **Technology:** AI algorithms create complex geometries that are difficult to manufacture using traditional methods, enhancing fuel efficiency and performance of aircraft parts.

3. AI-Optimized Tooling and Fixtures

Example: Siemens

- **Application:** Siemens uses AI to optimize the design and production of tooling and fixtures for industrial manufacturing processes.

- **Technology:** AI algorithms analyze production data and perform simulations to generate designs that improve efficiency and durability of tooling used in additive manufacturing and beyond.

4. Personalized Medical Implants

Example: axial3D

- **Application:** axial3D employs AI to develop personalized medical implants and surgical models using additive manufacturing.

- **Technology:** AI algorithms process medical imaging data (e.g., CT scans) to create precise 3D models of patient anatomy, enabling surgeons to plan and practice complex surgeries with accuracy.

5. AI-Driven Architectural Prototyping

Example: Branch Technology

- **Application:** Branch Technology utilizes AI and robotic 3D printing to create architectural prototypes and custom structures.

- **Technology:** AI algorithms optimize designs for structural integrity and aesthetics, facilitating the construction of complex geometries with minimal material waste.

6. AI-Powered Fashion and Wearables

Example: Ministry of Supply

- **Application:** Ministry of Supply integrates AI with 3D printing to develop personalized fashion and wearable products.

- **Technology:** AI algorithms analyze user data (e.g., body measurements, movement patterns) to create custom-fit clothing and accessories using additive manufacturing techniques.

7. Smart Manufacturing and IoT Devices

Example: Formlabs

- **Application:** Formlabs applies AI to enhance smart manufacturing capabilities and IoT (Internet of Things) devices.

- **Technology:** AI algorithms optimize production processes, monitor equipment performance, and enable predictive maintenance in additive manufacturing environments, improving operational efficiency and reliability.

8. Sustainable Consumer Goods

Example: adidas

- **Application:** adidas employs AI-driven design tools and 3D printing to create sustainable consumer goods, such as footwear and apparel.

- **Technology:** AI algorithms generate designs that minimize material waste and energy consumption, supporting adidas' sustainability goals while offering customizable products to consumers.

9. AI-Enhanced Educational Tools

Example: Ultimaker

- **Application:** Ultimaker integrates AI into educational 3D printing solutions, providing enhanced learning tools for schools and universities.

- **Technology:** AI algorithms support curriculum development and student projects by facilitating design optimization, simulation, and prototyping using additive manufacturing techniques.

10. AI-Optimized Food and Culinary Products

Example: Natural Machines (Foodini)

- **Application:** Natural Machines uses AI-powered 3D food printing technology to create customized culinary products.

- **Technology:** AI algorithms control the deposition of food ingredients, enabling personalized nutrition and creative culinary designs using additive manufacturing in the food industry.

These examples illustrate how AI is driving innovation and customization in additive manufacturing, transforming industries and expanding the possibilities of what can be achieved with 3D printing technology. As AI continues to evolve, its integration with additive manufacturing is expected to lead to further advancements in product design, manufacturing efficiency, and personalized consumer experiences.

AI – Applications and Concepts

In additive manufacturing (AM), AI (Artificial Intelligence) plays a crucial role in optimizing various stages of the manufacturing process, enhancing efficiency, quality, and customization capabilities. Here are key concepts of AI used in additive manufacturing:

1. Generative Design

Concept: Generative design involves using AI algorithms to explore a vast range of possible designs based on specified parameters and performance criteria. It allows for the creation of complex and optimized geometries that are well-suited for additive manufacturing processes.

Application: AI-driven generative design tools generate lightweight structures with minimal material usage, optimizing strength-to-weight ratios and overall part performance.

2. Machine Learning for Process Optimization

Concept: Machine learning algorithms analyze data from sensors and historical manufacturing processes to optimize additive manufacturing parameters in real-time. This includes adjusting temperature, speed, and material deposition rates for improved efficiency and quality.

Application: Predictive algorithms anticipate potential defects or deviations during printing, allowing for proactive adjustments and minimizing waste.

3. Quality Assurance and Defect Detection

Concept: AI-based computer vision systems analyze images and sensor data in real-time to detect defects, anomalies, or deviations during the additive manufacturing process.

Application: By continuously monitoring prints, AI can identify defects early, enabling immediate corrective actions and ensuring high-quality production without the need for human intervention.

4. Design Optimization and Personalization

Concept: AI algorithms analyze customer data, preferences, and requirements to generate personalized designs or adapt existing designs for additive manufacturing.

Application: This capability allows for mass customization, where each product can be tailored to individual specifications while optimizing performance and aesthetics.

5. Predictive Maintenance

Concept: AI predicts maintenance needs based on usage patterns, sensor data, and historical performance metrics of additive manufacturing equipment.

Application: By identifying potential equipment failures before they occur, AI-driven predictive maintenance minimizes downtime, improves operational efficiency, and extends the lifespan of machinery.

6. Material Selection and Development

Concept: AI algorithms analyze material properties, behavior under different conditions, and compatibility with additive manufacturing processes to optimize material selection.

Application: This includes developing new materials or composites tailored for specific applications, such as aerospace components or medical implants, based on performance requirements.

7. Smart Manufacturing and IoT Integration

Concept: AI integrates with IoT (Internet of Things) devices embedded within additive manufacturing equipment to create smart manufacturing environments.

Application: By collecting and analyzing real-time data from connected devices, AI optimizes production schedules, monitors equipment health, and enhances overall operational efficiency.

8. Simulation and Virtual Prototyping

Concept: AI-powered simulation tools predict and simulate additive manufacturing processes virtually, validating designs and identifying potential issues before physical production.

Application: This capability reduces prototyping costs and accelerates time-to-market by optimizing designs and verifying manufacturability without the need for extensive physical testing.

9. Supply Chain Optimization

Concept: AI optimizes supply chain management in additive manufacturing by forecasting demand, managing inventory levels, and identifying cost-effective sourcing options.

Application: This ensures timely availability of materials and components, reduces logistics costs, and minimizes supply chain disruptions.

10. Sustainability and Waste Reduction

Concept: AI algorithms optimize additive manufacturing processes to minimize material waste, energy consumption, and environmental impact.

Application: By optimizing designs for minimal material usage and energy efficiency, AI supports sustainable manufacturing practices and contributes to environmental conservation efforts.

These key concepts illustrate how AI enhances additive manufacturing capabilities across design, production, quality control, and sustainability, driving innovation and enabling new possibilities in manufacturing industries.

AI – Algorithms for Additive Manufacturing

AI algorithms play a significant role in enhancing additive manufacturing (AM) processes. Here is a list of key AI algorithms commonly used in various aspects of additive manufacturing:

1. Machine Learning Algorithms

1.1 Supervised Learning:

- **Linear Regression:** Predicts continuous outcomes, such as the optimal printing temperature or speed.

- **Support Vector Machines (SVM):** Classifies print quality or identifies defects based on sensor data.

- **Decision Trees and Random Forests:** Used for classification and regression tasks, such as predicting print success or material properties.

- **Neural Networks:** Deep learning models used for complex pattern recognition and prediction tasks, such as defect detection from images.

1.2 Unsupervised Learning:

- **K-Means Clustering:** Groups similar data points, such as categorizing different types of defects or print conditions.

- **Principal Component Analysis (PCA):** Reduces dimensionality of data, helping in visualizing and understanding high-dimensional sensor data.

1.3 Reinforcement Learning:

- **Q-Learning:** Optimizes printing parameters by learning from interactions with the manufacturing environment.

- **Deep Q-Networks (DQN):** Uses deep learning to handle more complex optimization problems in real-time process control.

2. Neural Networks and Deep Learning

2.1 Convolution Neural Networks (CNNs):

- **Image Recognition:** Identifies and classifies defects from real-time images of the printing process.

- **Pattern Recognition:** Analyzes layer-by-layer prints to ensure consistency and quality.

2.2 Recurrent Neural Networks (RNNs):

- **Time-Series Analysis:** Monitors and predicts the behavior of printing processes over time, such as temperature fluctuations or mechanical stresses.

2.3 Generative Adversarial Networks (GANs):

- **Design Generation:** Creates novel and optimized design patterns for additive manufacturing, enhancing creativity and efficiency.

3. Optimization Algorithms

3.1 Genetic Algorithms:

- **Optimization:** Evolves designs and process parameters to find optimal solutions for printing efficiency and part performance.

3.2 Particle Swarm Optimization (PSO):

- **Parameter Tuning:** Adjusts printing parameters dynamically to achieve optimal print quality and material usage.

4. Clustering and Dimensionality Reduction

4.1 K-Means Clustering:

- **Data Segmentation:** Groups similar patterns in sensor data, aiding in defect classification and process optimization.

4.2 Hierarchical Clustering:

- **Data Analysis:** Organizes data into a hierarchy of clusters, useful for understanding relationships in complex datasets.

5. Predictive Analytics

5.1 Bayesian Networks:

- **Uncertainty Modeling:** Predicts the likelihood of defects and failures based on probabilistic models of the manufacturing process.

5.2 Time Series Forecasting:

- **ARIMA (AutoRegressive Integrated Moving Average):** Predicts future trends in process parameters and equipment performance.

6. Anomaly Detection

6.1 Isolation Forest:

- **Outlier Detection:** Identifies unusual patterns in sensor data that may indicate defects or process anomalies.

6.2 Auto encoders:

- **Defect Detection:** Learns a compressed representation of the normal process data, detecting anomalies when the reconstruction error is high.

7. Natural Language Processing (NLP)

7.1 Text Mining:

- **Knowledge Extraction:** Analyzes technical documents, manuals, and logs to extract valuable insights for process improvement and troubleshooting.

Applications in Additive Manufacturing:

1. **Design Optimization:**

   o AI algorithms generate and refine design alternatives based on performance criteria and manufacturing constraints.

2. **Process Monitoring:**

   o Machine learning models analyze real-time sensor data to detect and correct anomalies during the printing process.

3. **Quality Control:**

   o Image recognition and anomaly detection algorithms ensure the printed parts meet quality standards.

4. **Predictive Maintenance:**

   o Predictive models forecast equipment failures, enabling proactive maintenance and reducing downtime.

5. **Material Development:**

   o   AI-driven simulations and optimizations assist in developing new materials with desired properties for specific applications.

The integration of these AI algorithms into additive manufacturing processes leads to enhanced efficiency, higher quality, and greater innovation in manufacturing practices.

AI – Case studies

Certainly! Here are some notable case studies demonstrating the integration of AI in 3D printing across various industries:

1. General Electric (GE) Aviation: AI for Predictive Maintenance and Quality Control

Context: GE Aviation utilizes AI and 3D printing to manufacture complex jet engine parts, such as fuel nozzles.

AI Application:

- **Predictive Maintenance:** GE uses machine learning algorithms to analyze sensor data from the printing process, predicting potential equipment failures and maintenance needs.

- **Quality Control:** Convolutional Neural Networks (CNNs) analyze images of each printed layer in real-time to detect defects early, ensuring high-quality parts.

Impact:

- Reduced maintenance downtime.

- Increased reliability and performance of 3D printed jet engine components.

- Enhanced defect detection accuracy, minimizing waste and rework.

2. Siemens: AI-Driven Design Optimization

Context: Siemens integrates AI with 3D printing to optimize the design and manufacturing of gas turbine blades.

AI Application:

- **Generative Design:** AI algorithms generate optimized blade designs that reduce weight while maintaining structural integrity.

- **Simulation and Validation:** Machine learning models simulate the performance of different designs under various operating conditions, ensuring optimal performance.

Impact:

- Significant weight reduction in turbine blades, leading to increased efficiency and reduced fuel consumption.

- Accelerated design cycle and reduced time-to-market for new turbine models.

3. Adidas: Custom-Fit Footwear with AI and 3D Printing

Context: Adidas leverages AI and 3D printing to produce customized athletic footwear, known as the Futurecraft 4D line.

AI Application:

- **Personalization:** AI algorithms analyze athlete foot scans and movement data to generate custom shoe designs tailored to individual users.

- **Production Optimization:** Machine learning models optimize the printing process to ensure consistent quality and efficient material usage.

Impact:

- Improved performance and comfort for athletes through custom-fit shoes.

- Enhanced customer satisfaction with personalized products.

- Streamlined manufacturing process, reducing production costs and waste.

4. Autodesk and Airbus: Generative Design for Aerospace Components

Context: Autodesk collaborates with Airbus to apply AI-driven generative design in creating lightweight, optimized components for aircraft.

AI Application:

- **Generative Design:** AI algorithms explore thousands of design permutations to produce components that are lighter and stronger than traditional designs.

- **Topology Optimization:** The designs are optimized for additive manufacturing, ensuring minimal material usage and maximum performance.

Impact:

- Significant weight reduction in aircraft components, leading to improved fuel efficiency.

- Enhanced design innovation and structural performance.

- Reduced environmental impact through material efficiency.

5. HP and Jabil: AI for Supply Chain and Production Optimization

Context: HP and Jabil use AI to enhance the efficiency and flexibility of their 3D printing supply chain and production processes.

AI Application:

- **Supply Chain Optimization:** AI models predict demand and optimize inventory management, ensuring timely availability of materials and parts.

- **Production Monitoring:** Machine learning algorithms analyze real-time data from 3D printers to optimize production parameters and ensure consistent quality.

Impact:

- Increased production efficiency and reduced lead times.

- Lowered inventory costs and minimized supply chain disruptions.

- Enhanced product quality and consistency.

6. Renishaw: AI in Metal 3D Printing for Medical Implants

Context: Renishaw employs AI to improve the design and production of metal 3D printed medical implants.

AI Application:

- **Design Optimization:** AI algorithms generate custom implant designs based on patient-specific anatomical data, improving fit and functionality.

- **Process Control:** Machine learning models monitor and control the metal 3D printing process to ensure precise material deposition and part quality.

Impact:

- Improved patient outcomes with custom-fitted implants.

- Reduced production time and costs for medical devices.

- Enhanced quality control, minimizing defects and rework.

7. BMW: AI-Enhanced Additive Manufacturing for Automotive Parts

Context: BMW integrates AI with 3D printing to produce complex automotive parts, such as lightweight brackets and customized interior components.

AI Application:

- **Topology Optimization:** AI algorithms optimize part geometries for strength and weight, reducing material usage while maintaining performance.

- **Defect Detection:** Computer vision systems powered by AI detect and correct defects during the printing process.

Impact:

- Lighter and more efficient automotive parts, contributing to overall vehicle performance.

- Reduced material costs and production time.

- Improved quality control and reduced waste.

These case studies illustrate the transformative potential of AI in enhancing 3D printing processes across various industries, driving innovation, efficiency, and customization while reducing costs and improving product quality.

8. BUSINESS MARKETING

Starting a business in additive manufacturing (AM) and marketing it effectively, even without prior experience, involves several strategic steps.

Get started:

1. Understand Your Market

Research the Industry:

- Identify key sectors that benefit from additive manufacturing (e.g., aerospace, healthcare, automotive, fashion).

- Study market trends, potential customers, and competitors.

Define Your Niche:

- Focus on a specific application or industry where you can offer unique value (e.g., custom medical implants, lightweight aerospace components, personalized consumer goods).

2. Build a Strong Brand

Create a Professional Image:

- Develop a compelling brand name, logo, and tagline.

- Design a professional website showcasing your services, case studies, and customer testimonials.

Establish Your Expertise:

- Share your knowledge about additive manufacturing through blog posts, whitepapers, and tutorials.

- Highlight any partnerships, certifications, or collaborations with industry experts.

3. Leverage Digital Marketing

Search Engine Optimization (SEO):

- Optimize your website with relevant keywords related to additive manufacturing.

- Create high-quality content that answers common questions and solves problems for your target audience.

Social Media Marketing:

- Use platforms like LinkedIn, Twitter, and Instagram to share updates, industry news, and your own content.

- Engage with potential customers and industry influencers by participating in discussions and groups.

Content Marketing:

- Produce educational content, such as blog posts, videos, webinars, and infographics.

- Share success stories and case studies demonstrating the impact of your 3D printing solutions.

4. Networking and Partnerships

Attend Industry Events:

- Participate in trade shows, conferences, and networking events related to additive manufacturing.

- Exhibit your products and services at relevant expos to attract potential customers.

Join Industry Associations:

- Become a member of professional organizations and trade associations in the additive manufacturing field.

- Leverage these networks to connect with potential partners and customers.

Collaborate with Other Businesses:

- Partner with companies that complement your services, such as material suppliers, software providers, or design firms.

- Offer joint solutions that provide added value to customers.

5. Showcase Your Work

Create a Portfolio:

- Display examples of your past projects and successful case studies on your website and social media.

- Highlight the benefits and unique aspects of your 3D printing solutions.

Offer Free Samples or Demonstrations:

- Provide potential customers with free samples or demonstrations to showcase the quality and capabilities of your additive manufacturing services.

6. Customer Engagement and Retention

Personalized Customer Service:

- Provide excellent customer support by being responsive and helpful.

- Tailor your services to meet the specific needs of each customer.

Gather and Showcase Testimonials:

- Request feedback and testimonials from satisfied customers.

- Display these testimonials prominently on your website and marketing materials.

Create Loyalty Programs:

- Offer discounts or incentives for repeat customers.

- Implement referral programs to encourage satisfied customers to refer new clients.

7. Leverage Online Marketplaces and Directories

List Your Business:

- Register your business on online directories and marketplaces that cater to additive manufacturing services (e.g., 3D Hubs, MakeXYZ).

- Ensure your profiles are complete and up-to-date with detailed descriptions of your services.

Utilize E-Commerce Platforms:

- If applicable, sell your 3D printed products through e-commerce platforms like Etsy, Amazon, or your own online store.

8. Continuous Learning and Adaptation

Stay Updated:

- Keep up with the latest advancements in additive manufacturing technology and industry trends.

- Continuously improve your skills and knowledge through online courses, certifications, and industry publications.

Adapt Your Strategy:

- Regularly review the performance of your marketing efforts using analytics tools.

- Be prepared to adjust your strategy based on what's working and what's not.

9. Utilize Paid Advertising

Google Ads and Social Media Ads:

- Run targeted ad campaigns on Google, LinkedIn, Facebook, and Instagram to reach specific demographics interested in additive manufacturing.

- Use precise targeting options to maximize your ad spend effectiveness.

Sponsored Content:

- Collaborate with industry blogs and influencers to create sponsored content that highlights your expertise and services.

Starting with these steps will help you build a solid foundation for marketing your additive manufacturing business. As you gain experience and insights, you can refine your strategies and explore new marketing channels to grow your business further.

Types of Business

There are various types of 3D modeling and print businesses, each catering to different industries and customer needs. Here are some common types of 3D printing businesses, along with brief descriptions of their focus areas:

1. Prototyping Services

Description:

- Offer rapid prototyping services to companies developing new products.

- Focus on creating functional prototypes to test form, fit, and function.

Target Industries:

- Consumer electronics, automotive, aerospace, medical devices, and consumer goods.

2. Custom Manufacturing

Description:

- Provide on-demand manufacturing for custom parts and small production runs.

- Specialize in creating unique or customized parts not feasible with traditional manufacturing methods.

Target Industries:

- Automotive, aerospace, industrial equipment, and personalized consumer products.

3. Medical and Dental Solutions

Description:

- Focus on creating custom medical devices, implants, dental prosthetics, and surgical guides.

- Use biocompatible materials and advanced 3D printing techniques.

Target Industries:

- Healthcare, dental clinics, hospitals, and medical research institutions.

4. Architectural Models

Description:

- Produce detailed architectural models for architects, builders, and real estate developers.

- Use 3D printing to create accurate scale models of buildings and structures.

Target Industries:

- Architecture, construction, real estate, and urban planning.

5. Jewelry and Fashion Accessories

Description:

- Design and print custom jewelry, fashion accessories, and wearable art.

- Offer personalized design services and use precious metals and high-quality materials.

Target Industries:

- Fashion, jewelry design, and luxury goods.

6. Education and Training

Description:

- Provide 3D printing services and training to educational institutions.

- Develop educational kits and materials to teach students about 3D printing technology.

Target Industries:

- Schools, universities, technical institutes, and educational programs.

7. Consumer Products

Description:

- Create custom and personalized consumer products such as phone cases, home decor, and toys.

- Utilize e-commerce platforms to sell directly to consumers.

Target Industries:

- Consumer goods, home decor, and gifts.

8. Art and Sculpture

Description:

- Produce custom art pieces, sculptures, and installations for artists and collectors.

- Collaborate with artists to bring their digital designs to life using 3D printing.

Target Industries:

- Art galleries, museums, artists, and collectors.

9. Automotive Parts and Accessories

Description:

- Manufacture custom automotive parts, accessories, and modifications.

- Focus on creating lightweight and high-performance components.

Target Industries:

- Automotive aftermarket, motorsports, and custom car enthusiasts.

10. Aerospace Components

Description:

- Develop and produce lightweight and high-strength components for the aerospace industry.

- Specialize in parts that require complex geometries and high-performance materials.

Target Industries:

- Aerospace, defense, and aviation.

11. Food and Culinary Printing

Description:

- Create custom food items and decorations using food-safe 3D printing technologies.

- Offer services to chefs, restaurants, and event planners.

Target Industries:

- Food and beverage, culinary arts, and event planning.

12. 3D Scanning and Modeling Services

Description:

- Provide 3D scanning and modeling services to create accurate digital representations of physical objects.

- Use these models for reverse engineering, digital archiving, or further 3D printing.

Target Industries:

- Manufacturing, heritage preservation, and digital archiving.

13. Industrial Tooling and Jigs

Description:

- Design and manufacture custom tooling, jigs, and fixtures for industrial applications.

- Focus on improving manufacturing efficiency and precision.

Target Industries:

- Manufacturing, automotive, and aerospace.

14. Bioprinting

Description:

- Develop and produce bioprinted tissues, organs, and medical research models.

- Utilize advanced biocompatible materials and techniques.

Target Industries:

- Medical research, pharmaceuticals, and healthcare.

15. Sustainability and Recycling

Description:

- Offer 3D printing services focused on sustainable practices and using recycled materials.

- Promote eco-friendly production methods and products.

Target Industries:

- Environmental organizations, green consumer products, and sustainable manufacturing.

Each of these business types leverages the capabilities of 3D printing technology to address specific market needs, offering unique value propositions to their target customers.

Ways to Enter into Market:

Entering the additive manufacturing (AM) business involves several strategic steps. Here's a comprehensive guide to help you get started:

1. Market Research and Business Plan

Conduct Market Research:

- Identify potential markets and industries that benefit from additive manufacturing (e.g., aerospace, healthcare, automotive).

- Analyze market trends, customer needs, and competitor landscape.

Create a Business Plan:

- Define your business model (e.g., service bureau, product development, custom manufacturing).

- Outline your value proposition, target market, marketing strategy, operational plan, and financial projections.

2. Choose Your Niche

Select a Focus Area:

- Decide on the specific applications or industries you want to target (e.g., prototyping, medical implants, custom jewelry).

- Choose a niche that aligns with your skills, interests, and market demand.

3. Acquire Knowledge and Skills

Learn About 3D Printing Technologies:

- Understand different 3D printing technologies (e.g., FDM, SLA, SLS, DMLS).

- Stay updated with the latest advancements and trends in the AM industry.

Gain Technical Skills:

- Take online courses, attend workshops, and participate in training programs to acquire hands-on experience with 3D printers and CAD software.

- Familiarize yourself with design principles for additive manufacturing.

4. Invest in Equipment and Software

Choose the Right 3D Printer:

- Select 3D printers based on your target applications, materials, and budget.

- Consider factors such as build volume, print quality, material compatibility, and reliability.

Acquire Design Software:

- Invest in CAD software for designing 3D models (e.g., Autodesk Fusion 360, SolidWorks, Blender).

- Utilize slicing software to prepare models for printing (e.g., Cura, PrusaSlicer).

5. Set Up Your Workspace

Create a Functional Workspace:

- Set up a dedicated area for your 3D printers, materials, and post-processing tools.

- Ensure a clean and well-ventilated environment to maintain print quality and safety.

6. Develop a Strong Online Presence

Build a Professional Website:

- Showcase your services, portfolio, and customer testimonials.

- Include detailed information about your capabilities, pricing, and contact details.

Leverage Social Media:

- Use platforms like LinkedIn, Instagram, and Facebook to promote your business and engage with potential customers.

- Share content such as project updates, case studies, and industry news.

7. Network and Collaborate

Attend Industry Events:

- Participate in trade shows, conferences, and networking events related to additive manufacturing.

- Connect with industry professionals, potential customers, and suppliers.

Join Industry Associations:

- Become a member of professional organizations and trade associations in the AM field.

- Leverage these networks to gain insights, resources, and business opportunities.

8. Offer Competitive Services

Provide Value-Added Services:

- Offer additional services such as design consultation, rapid prototyping, post-processing, and finishing.

- Ensure high-quality prints and reliable turnaround times.

Focus on Customer Satisfaction:

- Provide excellent customer support and maintain open communication with clients.

- Gather feedback and continuously improve your services.

9. Leverage E-Commerce and Online Marketplaces

Sell Online:

- List your products and services on e-commerce platforms (e.g., Etsy, Amazon) and online marketplaces for 3D printing (e.g., Shapeways, 3D Hubs).

- Ensure clear product descriptions, high-quality images, and competitive pricing.

10. Explore Funding Options

Seek Investment:

- Consider funding options such as bank loans, venture capital, crowdfunding, or government grants.

- Prepare a solid business plan and pitch to attract investors.

11. Stay Updated and Adapt

Keep Up with Industry Trends:

- Continuously learn about new technologies, materials, and applications in additive manufacturing.

- Adapt your business strategy to stay competitive and meet evolving customer needs.

12. Consider Strategic Partnerships

Collaborate with Other Businesses:

- Partner with companies that complement your services, such as material suppliers, design firms, or software providers.

- Offer joint solutions to provide added value to customers.

By following these steps, you can effectively enter the additive manufacturing business and build a successful venture. Focus on understanding your market, acquiring the necessary skills and equipment, and continuously improving your services to meet customer demands.

Successful Business with Additive Manufacturing

Success in the additive manufacturing (AM) business requires strategic planning, continuous learning, and a customer-centric approach. Here are key steps to help you build a successful AM business:

1. Understand the Market and Define Your Niche

Market Research:

- Identify high-demand sectors such as aerospace, healthcare, automotive, consumer goods, and industrial tooling.

- Analyze market trends, customer needs, and competitors.

Niche Selection:

- Choose a specific area of expertise where you can offer unique value, such as custom medical implants, rapid prototyping, or personalized consumer products.

2. Invest in Quality Equipment and Software

Choose the Right Technology:

- Select 3D printers and materials suited to your niche and customer requirements.

- Consider factors like print quality, build volume, material compatibility, and cost.

Software Tools:

- Invest in robust CAD software (e.g., Autodesk Fusion 360, SolidWorks) and slicing software (e.g., Cura, PrusaSlicer).

- Ensure your software choices can handle the complexity of your projects and streamline your workflow.

3. Develop Technical Expertise

Continuous Learning:

- Stay updated with the latest advancements in AM technologies, materials, and design techniques.

- Participate in workshops, online courses, and industry certifications.

Build a Skilled Team:

- Hire or train staff with expertise in 3D printing, CAD design, material science, and quality control.

- Foster a culture of continuous improvement and innovation within your team.

4. Focus on Quality and Reliability

Quality Control:

- Implement rigorous quality control processes to ensure high standards in every print.

- Use inspection tools and techniques to detect and correct defects early in the process.

Reliability:

- Maintain and calibrate your equipment regularly to minimize downtime and ensure consistent performance.

- Offer reliable delivery times and excellent customer service to build trust and repeat business.

5. Innovate and Differentiate

Product Innovation:

- Develop unique products or services that differentiate you from competitors.

- Use AI and generative design tools to create optimized and innovative designs.

Customization:

- Offer personalized solutions tailored to individual customer needs, such as custom-fit medical devices or bespoke consumer products.

6. Build Strong Relationships

Customer Relationships:

- Provide exceptional customer service and support.

- Engage with your customers to understand their needs and gather feedback for continuous improvement.

Partnerships:

- Collaborate with material suppliers, software providers, and other industry players to enhance your capabilities.

- Participate in industry networks and trade associations to expand your business contacts and opportunities.

7. Effective Marketing and Branding

Online Presence:

- Develop a professional website showcasing your services, case studies, and customer testimonials.

- Use SEO strategies to improve your visibility in search engines.

Content Marketing:

- Share valuable content such as blog posts, whitepapers, and video tutorials that demonstrate your expertise.

- Use social media platforms to engage with your audience and share industry news and updates.

Networking:

- Attend industry conferences, trade shows, and networking events to promote your business and connect with potential customers.

- Join online forums and groups related to additive manufacturing to increase your visibility and credibility.

8. Financial Management

Cost Control:

- Monitor your costs closely and look for ways to optimize your production process.

- Invest wisely in new technologies and equipment that offer a clear return on investment.

Funding and Investment:

- Seek funding options such as loans, grants, or venture capital to support your business growth.

- Prepare a solid business plan and financial projections to attract investors.

9. Adapt and Scale

Scalability:

- Develop scalable processes that allow you to handle increased production volumes without compromising quality.

- Invest in automation and efficient workflows to improve productivity.

Adaptability:

- Stay flexible and ready to adapt to changing market conditions and customer demands.

- Continuously innovate and explore new applications and markets for your 3D printing services.

10. Leverage Data and Analytics

Data-Driven Decisions:

- Use data analytics to monitor your production processes, quality control, and customer interactions.

- Make informed decisions based on data insights to improve efficiency and customer satisfaction.

Predictive Maintenance:

- Implement predictive maintenance strategies to prevent equipment failures and reduce downtime.

By following these strategies, you can build a successful additive manufacturing business that delivers high-quality products, meets customer needs, and stays ahead of the competition.

Online and Offline Marketing Tips

Marketing your additive manufacturing business effectively involves both online and offline strategies. Here are some tips to help you reach your target audience and grow your business:

Online Marketing Tips

1. **Build a Professional Website:**

   - Ensure your website is user-friendly, visually appealing, and mobile-responsive.

   - Include detailed information about your services, capabilities, and case studies.

   - Use high-quality images and videos of your 3D printed products.

2. **Search Engine Optimization (SEO):**

   o   Optimize your website content with relevant keywords related to additive manufacturing and your niche.

   o   Create informative blog posts, whitepapers, and case studies to attract organic traffic.

   o   Use meta tags, alt text for images, and internal linking to improve your site's SEO.

3. **Content Marketing:**

   o   Share valuable content such as tutorials, industry news, and success stories.

   o   Use blog posts, infographics, videos, and webinars to educate your audience.

   o   Offer downloadable resources like e-books and guides in exchange for contact information.

4. **Social Media Marketing:**

   o   Use platforms like LinkedIn, Instagram, Twitter, and Facebook to engage with your audience.

   o   Share updates, behind-the-scenes content, customer testimonials, and industry insights.

   o   Participate in relevant groups and discussions to increase your visibility and credibility.

5. **Email Marketing:**

   o   Build an email list by offering valuable content and incentives for sign-ups.

   o   Send regular newsletters with updates, special offers, and educational content.

- o Use personalized email campaigns to nurture leads and maintain customer relationships.

6. **Paid Advertising:**

   - o Use Google Ads to target specific keywords related to additive manufacturing.

   - o Run targeted ads on social media platforms to reach your ideal customer segments.

   - o Experiment with retargeting ads to bring back visitors who showed interest in your services.

7. **Online Marketplaces and Directories:**

   - o List your business on online directories and marketplaces such as 3D Hubs, Shapeways, and MakeXYZ.

   - o Ensure your profiles are complete with detailed descriptions, high-quality images, and customer reviews.

8. **Influencer and Partnership Marketing:**

   - o Collaborate with industry influencers and bloggers to promote your services.

   - o Partner with complementary businesses to offer joint solutions and co-marketing opportunities.

Offline Marketing Tips

1. **Networking Events and Trade Shows:**

   - o Attend industry conferences, trade shows, and networking events to connect with potential customers and partners.

   - o Exhibit your products and services at relevant expos to showcase your capabilities.

2. **Printed Marketing Materials:**

   o Create professional brochures, business cards, and flyers to distribute at events and meetings.

   o Ensure your printed materials highlight your unique selling points and contact information.

3. **Public Relations (PR):**

   o Write and distribute press releases about significant milestones, new services, or industry awards.

   o Reach out to industry publications and news outlets to feature your business.

4. **Workshops and Seminars:**

   o Host workshops and seminars to educate potential customers about additive manufacturing and your services.

   o Offer hands-on demonstrations and training sessions to showcase your expertise.

5. **Local Advertising:**

   o Advertise in local newspapers, magazines, and industry journals to reach your target audience.

   o Consider sponsoring local events or participating in community activities to increase your visibility.

6. **Customer Referral Program:**

   o Encourage satisfied customers to refer new clients by offering incentives such as discounts or free services.

   o Provide exceptional customer service to foster strong relationships and word-of-mouth marketing.

7. **Direct Mail Campaigns:**

   o   Send personalized letters or postcards to potential clients, highlighting your services and special offers.

   o   Include samples or small promotional items to make your mail stand out.

8. **Partnerships with Educational Institutions:**

   o   Collaborate with schools, universities, and technical institutes to offer educational programs and workshops.

   o   Provide 3D printing services for academic projects and research initiatives.

9. **Local Business Partnerships:**

   o   Partner with local businesses and organizations that complement your services.

   o   Offer bundled solutions or co-host events to reach a broader audience.

Combining Online and Offline Strategies

- **Integrated Campaigns:** Run coordinated marketing campaigns across online and offline channels for a cohesive message.

- **Consistent Branding:** Ensure your branding is consistent across all marketing materials and platforms.

- **Track and Analyze:** Use analytics tools to track the effectiveness of your marketing efforts and adjust your strategies accordingly.

- **Customer Engagement:** Engage with your audience both online and offline to build strong relationships and trust.

By combining these online and offline marketing strategies, you can effectively promote your additive manufacturing business, attract new customers, and grow your brand presence in the industry.

Business Scaling

Scaling your additive manufacturing (AM) business requires strategic planning, efficient processes, and a focus on growth opportunities. Here are steps to help you scale your AM business effectively:

1. Strengthen Your Foundation

Optimize Operations:

- Streamline your production processes to increase efficiency and reduce costs.

- Implement lean manufacturing principles to eliminate waste and improve workflow.

Quality Control:

- Establish robust quality control systems to ensure consistent product quality.

- Invest in quality assurance tools and training for your team.

2. Invest in Technology and Equipment

Upgrade Equipment:

- Invest in advanced 3D printers that offer higher productivity, larger build volumes, and better material capabilities.

- Consider multi-material and multi-color printers to expand your product offerings.

Adopt Automation:

- Implement automation solutions for repetitive tasks such as post-processing, material handling, and quality inspection.

- Use software solutions to automate order management, production scheduling, and customer communication.

Embrace New Technologies:

- Stay updated with the latest advancements in AM technologies, such as metal 3D printing, bioprinting, and hybrid manufacturing.

- Invest in research and development to explore new applications and materials.

3. Expand Your Market Reach

Diversify Offerings:

- Expand your product and service offerings to cater to new markets and industries.

- Explore opportunities in high-demand sectors such as aerospace, healthcare, automotive, and consumer goods.

Geographic Expansion:

- Enter new geographic markets by establishing local offices, partnerships, or distribution channels.

- Leverage online platforms to reach international customers and offer global shipping.

4. Build a Strong Team

Hire Skilled Professionals:

- Recruit talented professionals with expertise in additive manufacturing, materials science, design, and engineering.

- Provide continuous training and development opportunities to keep your team updated with industry trends.

Foster a Collaborative Culture:

- Encourage collaboration and innovation within your team.

- Create an environment that supports creativity and problem-solving.

5. Enhance Customer Experience

Personalized Solutions:

- Offer customized solutions tailored to individual customer needs.

- Use data analytics to understand customer preferences and provide personalized recommendations.

Customer Support:

- Provide excellent customer service and support throughout the entire customer journey.

- Implement a robust customer relationship management (CRM) system to track and manage customer interactions.

6. Leverage Data and Analytics

Data-Driven Decisions:

- Use data analytics to monitor key performance indicators (KPIs) such as production efficiency, quality rates, and customer satisfaction.

- Make informed decisions based on data insights to improve operations and drive growth.

Predictive Analytics:

- Implement predictive analytics to anticipate market trends, customer demands, and potential issues.

- Use predictive maintenance to reduce downtime and extend the lifespan of your equipment.

7. Expand Sales and Marketing Efforts

Digital Marketing:

- Invest in digital marketing strategies to increase your online presence and attract new customers.

- Use search engine optimization (SEO), pay-per-click (PPC) advertising, and social media marketing to reach your target audience.

Content Marketing:

- Create valuable content such as blog posts, case studies, videos, and webinars to educate and engage your audience.

- Share success stories and testimonials to build credibility and trust.

Sales Channels:

- Explore new sales channels such as e-commerce platforms, online marketplaces, and industry-specific portals.

- Develop a strong sales team to identify and pursue new business opportunities.

8. Form Strategic Partnerships

Collaborate with Industry Leaders:

- Partner with leading companies in the AM industry to leverage their expertise, resources, and networks.

- Collaborate on research and development projects to drive innovation.

Academic and Research Institutions:

- Work with universities and research institutions to stay at the forefront of technological advancements.

- Participate in collaborative research projects and industry consortiums.

9. Focus on Sustainability

Sustainable Practices:

- Implement sustainable manufacturing practices to reduce waste and energy consumption.

- Use eco-friendly materials and recycling programs to minimize your environmental impact.

Green Certifications:

- Obtain relevant certifications and comply with industry standards for sustainability.

- Promote your commitment to sustainability as a competitive advantage.

10. Monitor and Adapt

Continuous Improvement:

- Regularly review and assess your business processes to identify areas for improvement.

- Implement feedback loops to continuously improve your products and services.

Adapt to Market Changes:

- Stay agile and be prepared to adapt to changes in market conditions, customer demands, and technological advancements.

- Monitor industry trends and competitors to stay ahead of the curve.

By following these steps, you can effectively scale your additive manufacturing business, improve operational efficiency, expand your market reach, and drive sustainable growth.

Business Globalization

Globalizing your additive manufacturing (AM) business involves expanding your reach beyond your local market and establishing a presence in international markets. Here are steps to help you successfully globalize your AM business:

1. Market Research and Analysis

Identify Target Markets:

- Research potential international markets where there is a demand for your AM services.

- Consider factors such as market size, growth potential, competition, and regulatory environment.

Cultural and Economic Analysis:

- Understand the cultural, economic, and business practices of the target markets.

- Analyze the purchasing power, preferences, and needs of potential customers in these regions.

2. Develop a Global Strategy

Define Your Goals:

- Set clear objectives for your global expansion, such as revenue targets, market share, or brand recognition.

- Develop a timeline and milestones for entering and establishing in new markets.

Adapt Your Business Model:

- Tailor your products, services, and pricing strategies to meet the specific needs of each market.

- Consider offering localized versions of your products and services.

3. Build a Strong Online Presence

Multilingual Website:

- Develop a multilingual website to cater to different languages spoken in your target markets.

- Optimize your website for international SEO to improve visibility in local search engines.

Global E-Commerce:

- Use e-commerce platforms that support international sales, such as Shopify, Amazon, or your own online store.

- Ensure your website supports multiple currencies and international payment methods.

Digital Marketing:

- Implement global digital marketing campaigns, including SEO, PPC, social media, and content marketing.

- Utilize local social media platforms and online communities to reach your target audience.

4. Establish Local Partnerships

Local Distributors and Agents:

- Partner with local distributors, agents, or resellers who understand the local market and can help promote your products.

- Build strong relationships with local partners to ensure smooth market entry.

Collaborate with Local Businesses:

- Form partnerships with local businesses, suppliers, and service providers to enhance your capabilities and offerings.

- Co-create solutions that cater to local market needs.

5. Compliance and Legal Considerations

Understand Local Regulations:

- Research and comply with local laws and regulations related to additive manufacturing, including intellectual property, import/export restrictions, and safety standards.

- Ensure your products meet local certifications and standards.

Intellectual Property Protection:

- Protect your intellectual property by registering patents, trademarks, and copyrights in each target market.

- Work with legal experts to navigate the complexities of international IP laws.

6. Logistics and Supply Chain Management

Efficient Shipping and Distribution:

- Set up reliable logistics and distribution networks to ensure timely delivery of your products.

- Consider partnering with international shipping and logistics companies to handle your supply chain.

Local Manufacturing:

- Explore the possibility of setting up local manufacturing facilities or using contract manufacturers to reduce shipping costs and lead times.

- Consider additive manufacturing hubs or shared facilities in key regions.

7. Adapt Marketing and Sales Strategies

Localized Marketing Campaigns:

- Create marketing campaigns that resonate with local cultures and preferences.

- Use local influencers, industry events, and trade shows to promote your brand.

Sales Channels:

- Utilize both online and offline sales channels to reach a wider audience.

- Train your sales team to understand the unique needs and preferences of international customers.

8. Customer Support and Service

Multilingual Support:

- Provide customer support in the languages spoken in your target markets.

- Use local customer service teams or multilingual support tools to address customer queries and issues.

After-Sales Service:

- Offer reliable after-sales service, including maintenance, repair, and technical support.

- Establish local service centers or partner with local service providers.

9. Build a Global Brand

Consistent Branding:

- Maintain consistent branding across all markets while allowing for local adaptations.

- Communicate your brand values and unique selling propositions clearly.

Global PR and Media Relations:

- Engage with international media and PR agencies to build your brand's reputation globally.

- Share success stories, case studies, and news about your global expansion efforts.

10. Monitor and Adapt

Track Performance:

- Use analytics tools to monitor the performance of your global marketing and sales efforts.

- Analyze data to understand customer behavior, market trends, and the effectiveness of your strategies.

Continuous Improvement:

- Be prepared to adapt your strategies based on feedback and market dynamics.

- Continuously improve your products, services, and customer experience to meet the evolving needs of international markets.

By following these steps, you can successfully globalize your additive manufacturing business, reach new customers, and establish a strong presence in international markets.

Growth Rate of Additive Manufacturing Business

The additive manufacturing industry has shown robust growth over the past decade, and forecasts indicate continued expansion. Key growth indicators include:

- **Market Size:** The global additive manufacturing market size was valued at approximately USD 12 billion in 2020 and is projected to grow significantly in the coming years.

- **Compound Annual Growth Rate (CAGR):** Forecasts suggest a CAGR of around 20% to 25% from 2021 to 2028, driven by technological advancements and increasing adoption across industries.

- **Industry Applications:** Growth is particularly strong in aerospace, automotive, healthcare, and consumer goods sectors, where AM offers unique advantages in design flexibility, cost-effectiveness, and rapid prototyping.

- **Regional Expansion:** Emerging markets in Asia-Pacific and Latin America are witnessing rapid adoption of additive manufacturing technologies, contributing to global growth.

- **Investment and Innovation:** Continued investment in R&D, partnerships, and acquisitions by major players is fueling innovation and expanding market opportunities.

In summary, additive manufacturing is poised for significant growth driven by technological innovation, expanding applications, and a shift towards sustainable and efficient manufacturing practices across industries. Companies that embrace these trends and adapt to evolving market dynamics are likely to capitalize on the opportunities presented by additive manufacturing.

9. TOP – 10 INDUSTRY TYCOONS

Top 10 – Indian Companies

India has a rapidly growing additive manufacturing (AM) industry with several companies leading the way in various sectors. Here are ten of the top additive manufacturing companies in India:

1. **Intech Additive Solutions Pvt. Ltd.**

   - **Sector:** Aerospace, Automotive, Healthcare

   - **Description:** Intech is a pioneer in metal additive manufacturing in India, offering a range of solutions from software to hardware and printing services. They focus on aerospace, automotive, and medical applications.

2. **Imaginarium India Pvt. Ltd.**

   - **Sector:** Jewelry, Medical, Automotive, Engineering

   - **Description:** Imaginarium is one of the largest 3D printing companies in India, providing prototyping and production services across various industries including jewelry, medical, and automotive.

3. **Wipro 3D**

   - **Sector:** Aerospace, Industrial, Defense

   - **Description:** A division of Wipro Infrastructure Engineering, Wipro 3D specializes in metal additive manufacturing for aerospace, industrial, and defense applications. They offer end-to-end solutions including design, prototyping, and production.

4. **Objectify Technologies Pvt. Ltd.**

     o **Sector:** Aerospace, Automotive, Tooling

     o **Description:** Objectify Technologies provides 3D printing services for prototyping and production. They focus on aerospace, automotive, and tooling sectors, offering both metal and polymer printing capabilities.

5. **Adroitec Information Systems Pvt. Ltd.**

     o **Sector:** Engineering, Healthcare, Automotive

     o **Description:** Adroitec offers comprehensive 3D printing solutions, including hardware, software, and services. They serve industries like engineering, healthcare, and automotive with a strong focus on innovation and quality.

6. **Think3D**

     o **Sector:** Education, Medical, Industrial, Aerospace

     o **Description:** Think3D is a prominent player in the Indian 3D printing industry, offering a wide range of services from prototyping to mass production. They cater to various sectors including education, medical, and aerospace.

7. **3D Product Development Pvt. Ltd. (3DPD)**

     o **Sector:** Engineering, Healthcare, Consumer Goods

     o **Description:** 3DPD specializes in rapid prototyping and manufacturing using 3D printing technologies. They serve engineering, healthcare, and consumer goods sectors with high-quality, precise manufacturing solutions.

8. **Fracktal Works**

- o **Sector:** Education, Engineering, Consumer Products

- o **Description:** Fracktal Works is known for developing 3D printers and offering 3D printing services. They focus on education, engineering, and consumer product development, helping businesses and institutions innovate with 3D printing.

9. **Chizel Prints Manufacturing Pvt. Ltd.**

- o **Sector:** Engineering, Automotive, Consumer Goods

- o **Description:** Chizel offers digital manufacturing solutions including 3D printing, CNC machining, and injection molding. They cater to the engineering, automotive, and consumer goods sectors, providing end-to-end manufacturing services.

10. **Redington (India) Limited**

- o **Sector:** Industrial, Healthcare, Automotive, Aerospace

- o **Description:** Redington is a leading distributor of 3D printers and related technologies in India. They offer a wide range of AM solutions for industrial, healthcare, automotive, and aerospace applications.

These companies are driving the adoption of additive manufacturing in India, offering innovative solutions across various industries and contributing to the growth of the 3D printing ecosystem in the country.

Top 10 – Countries:

The additive manufacturing (AM) industry is growing globally, with several countries leading the way in adopting and advancing this technology across various sectors. Here are ten countries known for their strong additive manufacturing industries:

1. **United States**

   o The USA is a pioneer in additive manufacturing with a strong presence in aerospace, healthcare, automotive, and consumer goods sectors. Companies like GE Additive, Stratasys, and 3D Systems are key players.

2. **Germany**

   o Germany is at the forefront of industrial 3D printing, particularly in automotive, aerospace, and engineering sectors. Companies like EOS, Siemens, and Concept Laser (now part of GE Additive) are notable players.

3. **China**

   o China has rapidly expanded its additive manufacturing capabilities, focusing on industrial applications, consumer goods, and healthcare. Companies like Farsoon, UnionTech, and Shining 3D are leading the market.

4. **Japan**

   o Japan is known for its advanced manufacturing technologies, including additive manufacturing. Key sectors include automotive, electronics, and healthcare. Companies like Mitsubishi Heavy Industries and Canon are prominent.

5. **United Kingdom**

   o The UK has a strong presence in aerospace, automotive, and healthcare sectors using additive manufacturing. Companies like Renishaw and GKN Aerospace are notable for their contributions.

6. **France**

   o   France has a growing additive manufacturing sector with applications in aerospace, automotive, and medical industries. Companies like Prodways and Michelin are involved in innovative AM technologies.

7. **South Korea**

   o   South Korea is advancing in additive manufacturing, particularly in electronics, automotive, and consumer goods. Companies like 3D Systems Korea and Rokit Healthcare are making significant strides.

8. **Italy**

   o   Italy has a robust additive manufacturing industry with applications in fashion, automotive, and aerospace sectors. Companies like DWS Systems and CRP Group are prominent players.

9. **Netherlands**

   o   The Netherlands is known for its innovative approach to additive manufacturing, focusing on aerospace, healthcare, and maritime industries. Companies like Ultimaker and Additive Industries are leading the way.

10. **Sweden**

   o   Sweden has a strong presence in additive manufacturing, particularly in aerospace, automotive, and industrial sectors. Companies like Sandvik and Arcam (now part of GE Additive) are key players in the market.

These countries are driving the development and adoption of additive manufacturing technologies globally, leveraging their strengths in various industries to innovate and grow their economies.

Top 10 – Entrepreneurs:

INDIA: Identifying specific Indian entrepreneurs who have made significant contributions exclusively in the field of 3D modeling and printing can be challenging due to the relatively nascent stage of the industry in India compared to global markets. However, here are some notable figures and companies in India that have been instrumental in promoting and advancing 3D modeling and printing technologies:

1. **Abhijit Bhattacharya**

    o **Sector:** Co-founder of Divide By Zero Technologies

    o **Contribution:** Leading manufacturer of industrial-grade 3D printers in India, focusing on innovative technologies and applications.

2. **Aniket Deb**

    o **Sector:** Co-founder of Ethereal Machines

    o **Contribution:** Developed the Ethereal Halo, a hybrid manufacturing machine that combines additive and subtractive manufacturing technologies.

3. **Nitin Jain**

    o **Sector:** Founder of 3D Spectra Technologies LLP

    o **Contribution:** Established as a major provider of 3D printing services and solutions in India, offering a wide range of applications from prototyping to production.

4. **Ananda Kallugadde**

    o **Sector:** Co-founder of Fabheads Automation

    o **Contribution:** Specializes in automated composite manufacturing using 3D printing, serving industries such as aerospace, automotive, and defense.

5. **Kshitij Parab**

   - **Sector:** Co-founder of Supercraft3D

   - **Contribution:** Focuses on medical and healthcare applications of 3D printing, providing patient-specific solutions and prosthetics.

6. **Deepak Raj**

   - **Sector:** Founder of Objectify Technologies Pvt. Ltd.

   - **Contribution:** Offers advanced 3D printing and additive manufacturing solutions across various industries including aerospace, automotive, and healthcare.

7. **Sathish Kumar**

   - **Sector:** Founder of Bangalore Alpha Lab

   - **Contribution:** Provides access to 3D printing technology through a network of labs and workshops, promoting education and entrepreneurship in AM.

8. **Anand Prakash**

   - **Sector:** Founder of DesignTech Systems Ltd.

   - **Contribution:** Provides CAD/CAM/CAE and 3D printing solutions, supporting industries such as automotive, aerospace, and consumer products.

9. **Rajeev Lochan**

   - **Sector:** Founder of Objectify Technologies Pvt. Ltd.

   - **Contribution:** Specializes in metal 3D printing services, catering to industries like aerospace, automotive, and medical sectors.

10. **Raja Sekhar Upputuri**

   - **Sector:** Co-founder of think3D

   - **Contribution:** Offers a wide range of 3D printing services and solutions, focusing on education, healthcare, and industrial applications.

These entrepreneurs and companies are actively contributing to the growth and adoption of 3D modeling and printing technologies in India, across various sectors from industrial manufacturing to healthcare and education. Their innovations and leadership are crucial in shaping the future of additive manufacturing in the country.

WORLD: Identifying the top entrepreneurs in 3D modeling and printing can be subjective and may vary depending on criteria such as innovation, impact on the industry, and business success. Here are ten entrepreneurs who have made significant contributions to the field of 3D modeling and printing:

1. **Chuck Hull**

   - **Sector:** Co-founder of 3D Systems

   - **Contribution:** Inventor of stereolithography (SLA), one of the earliest 3D printing technologies.

2. **Bre Pettis**

   - **Sector:** Co-founder of MakerBot Industries

   - **Contribution:** Pioneer in desktop 3D printing, making it accessible to individuals and small businesses.

3. **Max Lobovsky**

   - **Sector:** Co-founder of Formlabs

   - **Contribution:** Developed the Form 1 SLA 3D printer, popularizing high-resolution desktop 3D printing.

4. **Avi Reichental**

   - **Sector:** Former CEO of 3D Systems

   - **Contribution:** Led 3D Systems through significant growth and innovation in industrial 3D printing technologies.

5. **Carl Bass**

   - **Sector:** Former CEO of Autodesk

   - **Contribution:** Expanded Autodesk's software offerings into 3D modeling and additive manufacturing with products like Autodesk Fusion 360.

6. **Jonathan Jaglom**

   - **Sector:** CEO of MakerBot Industries

   - **Contribution:** Led MakerBot's expansion and development of desktop 3D printing solutions.

7. **David Reis**

   - **Sector:** Former CEO of Stratasys

   - **Contribution:** Instrumental in Stratasys' growth and leadership in industrial 3D printing, including the merger with Objet.

8. **Ric Fulop**

   - **Sector:** Co-founder of Desktop Metal

   - **Contribution:** Innovator in metal 3D printing technology, aiming to make metal AM accessible for mass production.

9. **Shuji Hashimoto**

   - **Sector:** Co-founder of Carbon

o **Contribution:** Pioneered Continuous Liquid Interface Production (CLIP) technology for rapid, high-quality resin-based 3D printing.

10. **Hans Langer**

    o **Sector:** Founder of EOS GmbH

    o **Contribution:** Founded EOS, a leading provider of industrial 3D printing solutions, focusing on metal and polymer AM technologies.

These entrepreneurs have played pivotal roles in advancing 3D modeling and printing technologies, making significant impacts across various sectors from consumer products to aerospace and healthcare. Their innovations and leadership continue to shape the future of additive manufacturing.

Top 10 – Sectors

Identifying the top 10 3D print products can vary based on application, innovation, and impact. Here are ten notable 3D printed products that have demonstrated significant advancements and applications:

1. **Prosthetics and Orthotics**

   o Customized prosthetic limbs and orthotic devices tailored to individual needs, improving comfort and functionality.

2. **Dental Implants and Aligners**

   o 3D printed dental implants and clear aligners for precise fitting and improved patient outcomes in orthodontics and dental restoration.

3. **Aerospace Components**

- Lightweight and complex aerospace components, such as turbine blades and structural brackets, using advanced materials like titanium and composites.

4. **Automotive Parts**

   - Prototyping and production of automotive parts, including interior components, custom tooling, and even functional car parts like air intake manifolds.

5. **Fashion and Wearables**

   - Customized fashion accessories, jewelry, and wearables showcasing intricate designs and personalized styles not possible with traditional manufacturing methods.

6. **Medical Models and Surgical Guides**

   - Patient-specific anatomical models for surgical planning and training, as well as surgical guides for precise implant placements and complex procedures.

7. **Architectural Models**

   - Detailed architectural models and prototypes used for visualization, urban planning, and showcasing designs to clients and stakeholders.

8. **Art and Sculptures**

   - Complex and artistic sculptures, installations, and artwork created with intricate details and unique shapes enabled by 3D printing technology.

9. **Educational Tools and Prototypes**

   - Educational aids, prototypes, and models used in classrooms and research labs for STEM education, enhancing learning and experimentation.

10. **Consumer Electronics and Gadgets**

   o Customized and personalized consumer electronics accessories, housings for gadgets, and tech innovations, reflecting individual preferences and functionality needs.

These examples highlight the versatility and transformative potential of 3D printing across various industries, showcasing its ability to innovate and customize products efficiently and effectively.

Top 10 – Products

Recognizing the top 10 additive manufacturing (AM) products involves highlighting innovative applications and impactful advancements across various industries. Here are ten recognized additive manufacturing products that have made significant contributions:

1. **GE LEAP Fuel Nozzle**

   o **Sector:** Aerospace

   o **Description:** Additively manufactured fuel nozzles for the GE LEAP jet engine, reducing weight and improving fuel efficiency.

2. **Invisalign Aligners**

   o **Sector:** Healthcare (Orthodontics)

   o **Description:** Customized clear aligners made using 3D printing technology for orthodontic treatments, offering precise fit and comfort.

3. **Lockheed Martin's Satellite Fuel Tank**

   o **Sector:** Aerospace

   o **Description:** Additively manufactured satellite fuel tank using titanium, reducing weight and optimizing space payload.

4. **Nike Vapor Laser Talon Football Cleat**

   - o **Sector:** Sports (Footwear)

   - o **Description:** 3D printed football cleat designed for speed and agility, featuring lightweight and aerodynamic properties.

5. **Airbus A350 XWB Bracket**

   - o **Sector:** Aerospace

   - o **Description:** Additively manufactured titanium brackets for the Airbus A350 XWB aircraft, reducing weight and enhancing structural integrity.

6. **Bespoke Innovations Fairing**

   - o **Sector:** Healthcare (Prosthetics)

   - o **Description:** Customized prosthetic fairings for amputees, offering personalized aesthetics and comfort through 3D scanning and printing.

7. **BMW's i8 Roadster Roof Bracket**

   - o **Sector:** Automotive

   - o **Description:** Additively manufactured aluminum roof brackets for the BMW i8 Roadster, optimizing weight and performance.

8. **Stryker's Tritanium® In-Growth Technology**

   - o **Sector:** Healthcare (Orthopedics)

   - o **Description:** Additively manufactured porous structures for orthopedic implants, promoting bone growth and implant integration.

9. **Local Motors' Strati**

- o **Sector:** Automotive

- o **Description:** World's first 3D printed electric car, demonstrating rapid manufacturing capabilities and sustainability in automotive production.

10. **NASA's 3D Printed Habitat Challenge Structures**

- o **Sector:** Space Exploration

- o **Description:** Additively manufactured habitat structures designed for future space missions, showcasing AM's potential in extraterrestrial construction.

These examples illustrate the diverse applications and benefits of additive manufacturing across aerospace, healthcare, automotive, and other sectors, highlighting its role in innovation, customization, and efficiency in manufacturing processes.

Top 10 – Services:

Identifying the top services in the additive manufacturing (AM) business involves recognizing companies and providers that offer innovative and impactful solutions across various sectors. Here are ten top services commonly offered in the additive manufacturing industry:

1. **Prototyping Services**

- o Rapid prototyping using 3D printing technologies to quickly produce prototypes for design validation and testing.

2. **Production Manufacturing**

- o Additive manufacturing for end-use production parts, including batch production and on-demand manufacturing.

3. **Customized Manufacturing**

- o Tailored solutions for personalized and customized products, catering to individual customer specifications and requirements.

4. **Material Development and Testing**

   - o Research and development of new materials for 3D printing, along with testing and validation of material properties.

5. **Design and Engineering Services**

   - o CAD design, engineering analysis, and optimization services to prepare models for additive manufacturing processes.

6. **Post-Processing and Finishing**

   - o Finishing services such as polishing, painting, and surface treatment to enhance the appearance and functionality of 3D printed parts.

7. **Consulting and Training**

   - o Consulting services for AM strategy development, implementation, and integration into existing manufacturing workflows. Training programs for operators and engineers.

8. **On-Demand Services**

   - o Online platforms and marketplaces offering on-demand 3D printing services, connecting customers with AM service providers globally.

9. **Reverse Engineering**

   - o 3D scanning and reverse engineering services to create digital models from physical objects, enabling replication or modification using additive manufacturing.

10. **Bio printing and Medical Solutions**

   o Services focused on bio printing for tissue engineering, personalized medicine, and medical device manufacturing using additive manufacturing technologies.

These services are essential in supporting the adoption and growth of additive manufacturing across industries, providing solutions from rapid prototyping to production-scale manufacturing and specialized applications like bio printing.

10. BUSINESS COMMERCIALIZATION

Commercializing an additive manufacturing (AM) business involves several critical steps to ensure success and sustainability in the market. Here's a detailed outline of the typical steps involved:

1. Market Research and Planning

- **Identify Market Opportunities:** Conduct thorough market research to identify target industries, potential customers, and competitors in the additive manufacturing space.

- **Define Value Proposition:** Clearly articulate what sets your AM business apart, whether it's specialized capabilities, materials expertise, cost-effectiveness, or rapid prototyping capabilities.

- **Business Plan Development:** Create a comprehensive business plan outlining your business objectives, target market segments, pricing strategies, sales and marketing plans, and financial projections.

2. Legal and Regulatory Considerations

- **Business Entity Formation:** Decide on the legal structure (e.g., LLC, corporation) and register your business according to local laws and regulations.

- **Intellectual Property Protection:** Assess and protect your intellectual property rights related to proprietary technologies, materials, or processes used in your additive manufacturing operations.

- **Compliance and Standards:** Understand and comply with industry standards, safety regulations, and environmental requirements applicable to additive manufacturing processes.

3. Infrastructure and Technology Setup

- **Equipment and Technology Selection:** Invest in suitable additive manufacturing equipment and software tailored to your business needs and target applications.

- **Facility Setup:** Establish a production facility or workspace equipped with necessary infrastructure, including power supply, ventilation, and safety measures for additive manufacturing operations.

- **Supply Chain Management:** Establish relationships with suppliers for materials, consumables, and post-processing services required for additive manufacturing processes.

4. Product Development and Prototyping

- **Design Capabilities:** Develop or partner with design engineers to offer design services or support customers in optimizing designs for additive manufacturing.

- **Prototyping Services:** Offer rapid prototyping services to allow customers to validate designs and iterate quickly before moving to full-scale production.

5. Quality Control and Assurance

- **Quality Management System:** Implement a robust quality management system to ensure consistency and reliability in 3D printed products.

- **Testing and Validation:** Conduct rigorous testing and validation of materials and finished parts to meet industry standards and customer specifications.

6. Sales and Marketing Strategy

- **Targeted Marketing Campaigns:** Develop targeted marketing strategies to reach potential customers through digital marketing, industry events, and networking.

- **Sales Channels:** Identify and establish sales channels, whether direct sales, partnerships with resellers, or online platforms, to reach your target market effectively.

- **Customer Relationships:** Build strong relationships with customers through exceptional service, responsiveness, and customized solutions.

7. Scaling and Growth

- **Operational Scaling:** Plan for scalability of operations by optimizing workflows, increasing production capacity, and expanding service offerings.

- **Investment and Funding:** Explore funding options such as loans, grants, or venture capital to support business growth, equipment upgrades, and market expansion.

- **Continuous Innovation:** Stay abreast of technological advancements in additive manufacturing and invest in R&D to innovate new products and services.

8. Risk Management and Sustainability

- **Risk Assessment:** Identify potential risks such as supply chain disruptions, regulatory changes, or technological obsolescence, and develop mitigation strategies.

- **Sustainability Practices:** Adopt sustainable practices in additive manufacturing operations, including material recycling, energy efficiency, and waste reduction initiatives.

9. Customer Feedback and Iteration

- **Continuous Improvement:** Gather customer feedback and iterate on products and services based on market demands and evolving customer needs.

- **Long-term Strategy:** Develop a long-term strategic roadmap for your additive manufacturing business, incorporating feedback, market trends, and technological advancements.

By following these steps, you can effectively commercialize your additive manufacturing business, establish a strong market presence, and position yourself for sustained growth and success in the dynamic additive manufacturing industry.

Business and Consumer Reach:

Reaching both businesses and consumers with your additive manufacturing products and services requires a strategic approach that addresses the unique needs and preferences of each group. Here are some tips to effectively reach both business clients and consumers:

1. Identify Target Audiences

- **Segmentation:** Segment your target audiences based on demographics, industries, and specific needs related to additive manufacturing products and services.

- **Persona Development:** Create buyer personas for businesses (B2B) and consumers (B2C) to understand their pain points, motivations, and decision-making criteria.

2. Tailored Messaging and Value Proposition

- **Business Clients (B2B):**

    - Highlight cost savings, efficiency improvements, and customization capabilities of your additive manufacturing solutions.

    - Emphasize ROI, scalability, and partnership benefits for integrating AM into their production processes.

- **Consumers (B2C):**

- Showcase customization options, unique designs, and personalization capabilities of your 3D printed products.

- Appeal to emotional factors such as novelty, personal expression, and sustainability aspects of AM products.

3. Effective Marketing Strategies

- **Digital Marketing:**

  - **Website Optimization:** Ensure your website is informative, user-friendly, and optimized for search engines (SEO) to attract organic traffic.

  - **Content Marketing:** Create valuable content (blogs, case studies, videos) that educates and engages your target audiences about AM applications and benefits.

  - **Social Media:** Use platforms like LinkedIn for B2B engagement and platforms like Instagram and Pinterest for B2C showcasing visual appeal and product features.

- **Offline Marketing:**

  - **Industry Events:** Participate in trade shows, conferences, and industry events to network with potential B2B clients and showcase your capabilities.

  - **Local Events:** Attend craft fairs, maker markets, and community events to promote B2C products and engage with local consumers.

4. Networking and Partnerships

- **B2B Relationships:**

  - Build relationships with industry associations, manufacturers, and businesses that can benefit from your additive manufacturing services.

- o Collaborate with complementary businesses (e.g., designers, engineers) to offer integrated solutions or joint marketing efforts.

- **B2C Engagement:**

  - o Partner with influencers or brand ambassadors in niches relevant to your consumer products to expand reach and credibility among target audiences.

  - o Foster community engagement through workshops, demonstrations, or online forums where consumers can learn about and interact with your AM products.

5. Customer Education and Support

- **B2B Clients:**

  - o Provide educational resources, workshops, or webinars to demonstrate the capabilities and ROI of AM for specific industries or applications.

  - o Offer technical support, training programs, and ongoing consultation to help businesses integrate AM into their operations effectively.

- **B2C Consumers:**

  - o Educate consumers about the benefits of 3D printing, material options, and customization possibilities through informative content and product demonstrations.

  - o Provide responsive customer support channels to address inquiries, facilitate orders, and ensure satisfaction with purchased products.

6. Feedback and Continuous Improvement

- **Collect Feedback:** Regularly gather feedback from both B2B clients and B2C consumers to understand their experiences, preferences, and suggestions for improvement.

- **Iterate and Innovate:** Use customer insights and market feedback to continuously refine your products, services, and marketing strategies to better meet the needs and expectations of your target audiences.

By implementing these strategies tailored to both business clients and consumers, you can effectively reach and engage your target audiences, build lasting relationships, and drive growth for your additive manufacturing products and services.

Corporate Client:

Approaching corporate clients for your 3D print business requires a strategic and targeted approach to demonstrate the value of your additive manufacturing (AM) products and services. Here are several effective ways to approach corporate clients:

1. Research and Targeting

- **Identify Target Industries:** Conduct thorough research to identify industries that can benefit most from your 3D printing solutions, such as aerospace, automotive, healthcare, or consumer goods.

- **Prospect Identification:** Create a list of potential corporate clients based on industry relevance, company size, and existing use of additive manufacturing technologies.

2. Value Proposition Development

- **Customized Solutions:** Tailor your value proposition to address specific pain points or challenges faced by each corporate client. Highlight how your 3D print solutions can offer cost savings, efficiency improvements, or innovation opportunities.

- **ROI and Benefits:** Clearly articulate the return on investment (ROI) and tangible benefits of using your AM services, such as faster prototyping, reduced material waste, or customized product development.

3. Networking and Relationship Building

- **Industry Events:** Attend trade shows, conferences, and networking events attended by corporate decision-makers in target industries. Use these opportunities to showcase your capabilities and build relationships.

- **LinkedIn and Professional Networks:** Connect with key decision-makers on LinkedIn and engage in industry-specific groups or forums to establish credibility and initiate conversations.

4. Direct Outreach and Cold Calling

- **Personalized Outreach:** Craft personalized emails or LinkedIn messages highlighting your understanding of their industry challenges and how your AM solutions can provide value.

- **Cold Calling:** Prepare a compelling elevator pitch that succinctly communicates your offerings and benefits. Follow up with targeted emails or meetings to discuss potential collaboration.

5. Educational Workshops and Webinars

- **Industry Education:** Offer educational workshops, webinars, or lunch-and-learn sessions to educate corporate clients about the capabilities and applications of additive manufacturing in their specific industry.

- **Demonstrations:** Conduct live demonstrations of your 3D printing technologies and showcase case studies or success stories relevant to their industry to illustrate real-world applications.

6. Pilot Projects and Proof of Concept

- **Pilot Programs:** Propose pilot projects or proof-of-concept trials to demonstrate the feasibility and benefits of your AM solutions without significant initial investment.

- **Risk Mitigation:** Offer assurances and risk-sharing agreements to mitigate concerns about adopting new technologies, showcasing your commitment to their success.

7. Collaboration and Partnerships

- **Collaborative Projects:** Seek opportunities for collaborative projects or joint ventures where your 3D print capabilities can complement their existing operations or product development initiatives.

- **Supplier Diversity Programs:** If applicable, highlight your status as a minority-owned, woman-owned, or small business enterprise to leverage supplier diversity programs that prioritize partnerships with diverse suppliers.

8. Continuous Engagement and Follow-Up

- **Relationship Building:** Foster ongoing communication and relationship-building efforts with corporate clients. Stay engaged through updates on industry trends, new technologies, or relevant case studies.

- **Feedback and Adaptation:** Solicit feedback from clients to continuously improve your offerings and adapt to their evolving needs, ensuring long-term satisfaction and partnership.

By leveraging these strategies, you can effectively approach corporate clients for your 3D print business, establish meaningful relationships, and position your company as a valuable partner in their additive manufacturing initiatives.

LEARNING RESOURCES

1. **Online Courses and Tutorials**
   - o Platforms like Coursera, Udemy, and LinkedIn Learning offer courses on CAD design, 3D printing technology, and business management.
   - o **Coursera, Udemy, LinkedIn Learning**: Offer courses on CAD software, slicing software, and 3D modeling.
   - o **YouTube**: Numerous tutorials for specific software tools and techniques.
   - o **YouTube Channels**: Channels like "Thomas Sanladerer," "Maker's Muse," and "3D Printing Nerd" offer tutorials and tips on 3D printer hardware.
   - o **MOOCs**: Platforms like Coursera and Udemy offer courses on 3D printing and hardware maintenance.

2. **Books and Publications**
   - o Books such as "The Zombie Apocalypse Guide to 3D Printing" by Clifford T. Smyth and "Additive Manufacturing Technologies" by Ian Gibson provide valuable insights into the field.
   - o **"Mastering CAD/CAM" by Ibrahim Zeid**: Comprehensive guide to CAD and CAM principles.
   - o **"3D Printing Failures" by Sean Aranda**: Troubleshooting guide for common 3D printing issues.

3. **Industry Certifications**
   - o Certifications from organizations like SME (Society of Manufacturing Engineers) and ASME (American

Society of Mechanical Engineers) can enhance credibility and expertise.

4. **Workshops and Conferences**
    o   Attending industry conferences, workshops, and trade shows can provide networking opportunities and stay updated on the latest advancements.
    o   **Hands-On Learning**: Joining local maker spaces or attending workshops can provide practical, hands-on experience with different types of 3D printers and post-processing techniques.

5. **Software-Specific Documentation**
    o   **Official Documentation**: Manuals and guides provided by software developers (e.g., Autodesk, Ultimaker).

6. **Community Forums and Groups**
    o   **Reddit, Facebook Groups, Online Forums**: Communities where you can ask questions and share knowledge.
    o   **Online Communities**: Platforms like Reddit, Facebook groups, and dedicated 3D printing forums provide support and advice from experienced users.

7. **Manufacturer Manuals and Documentation**
    o   **Official Guides**: Manuals and troubleshooting guides provided by printer manufacturers (e.g., Ultimaker, Prusa, Formlabs) are invaluable resources.

8. **Hands-On Practice**
    o   **Projects**: Work on personal or client projects to apply your skills in real-world scenarios.

- o **Internships and Apprenticeships**: Gain practical experience in a professional setting.

9. **Certification Programs**

   - o **Certifications**: Obtain certifications from recognized organizations to validate your skills (e.g., Autodesk Certified Professional).

10. **Personal Projects**

    - o **DIY Projects**: Building and modifying your own 3D printers can provide invaluable hands-on experience.

    - o **Client Projects**: Working on projects for clients helps refine your skills and understand real-world applications and requirements.

11. **Internships and Apprenticeships**

    - o **Industry Experience**: Gaining experience through internships or apprenticeships in established AM businesses can provide practical insights and professional networking opportunities.

REFERENCES

1. https://www.twi-global.com/technical-knowledge/faqs/what-is-additive-manufacturing
2. https://www.diabatix.com
3. https://markforged.com/resources/blog/additive-manufacturing-101-guide-the-basics
4. https://www.freepik.com/
5. https://www.medicaldesignandoutsourcing.com/best-applications-3d-printing-medical-industry/
6. https://3dx.ae/blogs/2023/12/3d-printing-vs-traditional-manufacturing/
7. https://www.shopify.com/blog/how-to-make-money-3d-printing
8. https://additive-x.com/blog/3d-printing-workflow-the-5-steps-explaned/
9. https://www.additivemanufacturing.media/kc/what-is-additive-manufacturing/additive-manufacturing-workflow
10. https://openai.com/

www.ingramcontent.com/pod-product-compliance
Lightning Source LLC
Chambersburg PA
CBHW041312120726
48005CB00014B/1968